Informing the legislative debate since 1914 _____

U.S.-Taiwan Relationship: Overview of Policy Issues

Shirley A. Kan
Specialist in Asian Security Affairs

Wayne M. Morrison
Specialist in Asian Trade and Finance

November 18, 2013

Congressional Research Service

7-5700

www.crs.gov

R41952

Summary

The purpose and scope of this CRS report is to provide a succinct overview with analysis of the major issues in the U.S. policy on Taiwan. This report will be updated as warranted. Taiwan formally calls itself the sovereign Republic of China (ROC), tracing its political lineage to the ROC set up after the revolution in 1911 in China. The ROC government retreated to Taipei in 1949. The United States recognized the ROC until the end of 1978 and has maintained a non-diplomatic relationship with Taiwan after recognition of the People's Republic of China (PRC) in Beijing in 1979. The State Department claims an "unofficial" U.S. relationship with Taiwan, despite official contacts that include arms sales. The Taiwan Relations Act (TRA) of 1979, P.L. 96-8, has governed policy in the absence of a diplomatic relationship or a defense treaty. Other key statements that guide policy are the three U.S.-PRC Joint Communiqués of 1972, 1979, and 1982; as well as the "Six Assurances" of 1982. (See also CRS Report RL30341, *China/Taiwan: Evolution of the "One China" Policy—Key Statements from Washington, Beijing, and Taipei.*)

For decades, Taiwan has been of significant security, economic, and political interest to the United States. In 2012, Taiwan was the 11th-largest U.S. trading partner. Taiwan is a major innovator and producer of information technology (IT) products, many of which are assembled in the PRC by Taiwan-invested firms there. Ties or tension across the Taiwan Strait affect international security (with potential U.S. intervention), the U.S.-Taiwan relationship, and U.S.-PRC cooperation. While the United States does not diplomatically recognize Taiwan, it is in reality an important autonomous actor. Today, 22 countries have diplomatic relations with Taiwan as the ROC. Taiwan's 23 million people enjoy self-governance with democratic elections. After Taiwan's presidential election in 2008, the United States congratulated Taiwan as a "beacon of democracy." Democracy has offered Taiwan's people a greater say in their status, given competing politics about Taiwan's national identity and priorities. Taiwan held presidential and legislative elections in January 2012. Kuomintang (KMT), or Nationalist Party, President Ma Ying-jeou won re-election against the Democratic Progressive Party's (DPP's) candidate.

Since Taiwan and the PRC resumed their quasi-official dialogue in 2008 under President Ma and cross-strait tension decreased, some have stressed the need to take steps by the United States and by Taiwan to strengthen their relationship to advance U.S. interests. Another approach has viewed closer cross-strait engagement as allowing U.S. attention to shift to expand cooperation with a rising China, which opposes U.S. arms sales and other dealings with Taiwan. In any case, Washington and Taipei have put more efforts into their respective relations with Beijing, while contending that they have pursued a positive, parallel U.S.-Taiwan relationship.

Taiwan's President Ma Ying-jeou has sought U.S. support for his policies, including Taiwan's inclusion in the U.S. Visa Waiver Program (VWP) (in 2012), the International Civil Aviation Organization (ICAO), and talks on maritime disputes in the East and South China Seas. Other policy issues include whether to approve arms sales, whether to restart U.S. Cabinet-level visits, and how to bolster trade relations and resolve disputes, such as through the Trade and Investment Framework Agreement (TIFA) talks (resumed in March 2013). The United States has been especially concerned about Taiwan's restrictions on U.S. beef and pork, even as Taiwan has claimed attention to international organizations and standards. Since March 2013, Chairmen Ed Royce and Robert Menendez of the House Foreign Affairs and Senate Foreign Relations Committees, and other Members, have supported a bilateral investment agreement (BIA). Legislation in the 113th Congress includes H.R. 419, H.R. 772, H.R. 1151 (P.L. 113-17), H.R. 1960, H.R. 3470, H.Con.Res. 29, H.Con.Res. 46, H.Con.Res. 55, H.Res. 185, S. 12, S. 579, S. 1197, S. 1683, and S.Res. 167. Other congressional actions have focused on arms sales. (See CRS Report RL30957, *Taiwan: Major U.S. Arms Sales Since 1990.*)

Contents

Figures

Tables

Contacts

Overview: Policy Interests and Issues

The purpose and scope of this CRS report is to provide a succinct overview with analysis of the major issues in the U.S. policy on Taiwan. Taiwan has been of significant security, economic, and political interest to the United States. While the United States does not diplomatically recognize Taiwan, it is in reality an important autonomous actor in the world. Today, 22 countries including the Vatican have diplomatic relations with Taiwan as the Republic of China (ROC).[1] In what many consider as a model democracy, Taiwan's 23 million people enjoy self-governance with democratic elections. In 2012, Taiwan was the 11th-largest U.S. trading partner. It is the 7th-largest market for U.S. agricultural products. Taiwan also is a major recipient of U.S. arms sales.

With active congressional involvement, the United States has played critical roles in Taiwan's economic development, political liberalization from an authoritarian dictatorship to a dynamic democracy, self-defense against the People's Republic of China's (PRC's) military threats, and preservation of international space. Overall, U.S. policy seeks to support security, political, and economic interests that involve peace and stability, the status quo in the Taiwan Strait, Taiwan's efforts to maintain international space, democracy and human rights in Taiwan, and U.S. businesses in Taiwan. As a critical concern, the United States has interests in the ties or tension across the Taiwan Strait, which affect international security (with potential U.S. intervention), the U.S.-Taiwan relationship, and U.S.-PRC cooperation. The cross-strait relationship has grown closer since the 1980s. When James Lilley arrived as the U.S. representative in Taipei in 1982, he was one of the first officials to encourage cross-strait economic ties as the driver in a trend toward greater peace and security.[2] Indeed, closer economic engagement gradually has increased regular contacts and reduced tension across the Taiwan Strait.

U.S. support for Taiwan has posed challenges to U.S. engagement with the PRC, though Washington and Beijing have advanced an overall cooperative relationship since the 1970s. As Washington has engaged with both Taipei and Beijing, long-standing issues for policy have included how to balance U.S. relations with Taiwan and with the PRC, and also how to balance maintaining the relationship with Taipei in its own right as opposed to approaching Taiwan as part of Washington's relationship with Beijing. For decades, Taipei has harbored fears about whether Beijing's cooperation with Washington has occurred at the expense of Taiwan's interests. U.S. policy seeks a cooperative relationship with a rising PRC, which opposes U.S. arms sales and other official dealings with Taiwan as interference in its internal affairs in unifying with Taiwan as a part of China. In an apparent contradiction, Beijing also seeks its preferred U.S. policies to influence Taiwan. However, Taiwan considers itself a sovereign country. As Taiwan shifted from an authoritarian political system, U.S. policy has been mindful of respecting its democracy.

After the Kuomintang (KMT) Party's Ma Ying-jeou became president in Taiwan in May 2008, he promptly resumed the dialogue across the Taiwan Strait after its suspension for a decade. The PRC had accused his predecessor, the Democratic Progressive Party's (DPP's) Chen Shui-bian, of pushing for de jure independence of Taiwan. The resumption of the cross-strait dialogue resulted in even closer economic engagement between Taiwan and the PRC as well as a reduction of

---

[1] Kiribati, Marshall Islands, Nauru, Palau, Solomon Islands, Tuvalu, Belize, Dominican Republic, El Salvador, Guatemala, Haiti, Honduras, Nicaragua, Panama, Paraguay, Saint Kitts and Nevis, Saint Lucia, Saint Vincent and Grenadines, Burkina Faso, Sao Tome and Principe, Swaziland, and Vatican. In 2007, Malawi switched diplomatic recognition from the ROC to the PRC. On November 14, 2013, Gambia ended its diplomatic recognition of the ROC.

[2] James Lilley with Jeffrey Lilley, *China Hands* (New York: Public Affairs, 2004).

tension, which was welcomed by the United States. This situation afforded U.S. policy opportunities to strengthen the U.S.-Taiwan relationship and/or shift attention to seek greater cooperation from Beijing. President Ma Ying-jeou has sought U.S. support, including arms sales, for Taiwan's stronger position to sustain cross-strait talks. One view has stressed that the United States and Taiwan needed to strengthen their relationship to pursue U.S. interests. Another approach has stressed that the new era of cross-strait engagement allowed for improved U.S. ties with a rising China and that Taiwan has pursued its own interests in engaging with the PRC. In any case, Washington and Taipei have put more efforts into their respective relations with Beijing, while contending that they have pursued a parallel, positive U.S.-Taiwan relationship.

On October 4, 2011, the House Foreign Affairs Committee held a hearing on "Why Taiwan Matters." Assistant Secretary of State Kurt Campbell testified that the United States sought a strategic "rebalancing" (or "pivot") of comprehensive priorities to focus more on the Asia-Pacific region. He stated that "a critical part of that overarching strategy is building a comprehensive, durable, and unofficial relationship between the United States and Taiwan." Campbell stressed that "the bedrock of that relationship is our security relationship." He called the Taiwan Relations Act (TRA) one of the most important acts of "legislative leadership" and foreign policy in U.S. history. He recognized that the TRA stipulates that the United States must maintain the capacity to resist coercion, maintain peace and stability, and provide necessary defense articles to Taiwan. He acknowledged that the Administration must "consult actively on Capitol Hill." Campbell also reaffirmed that the Six Assurances as well as the TRA and three U.S.-PRC Joint Communiques form the foundation of U.S. policy on Taiwan.

Overall, some salient issues for policy include the following:

- How effectively is the Administration encouraging Taiwan to support U.S. interests in peace and prosperity, including in U.S. alliances and the cross-strait relationship? Is the Administration effectively influencing Taiwan to play a helpful, stabilizing role in maritime disputes in the East and South China Seas?

- How might Congress exercise its roles in U.S. policy or engage with Taiwan? How might Congress ensure momentum in strengthening U.S.-Taiwan ties?

- Should the United States sell more weapons and which ones, as requested by Taiwan for its self-defense? How effectively is the Administration encouraging Taiwan to strengthen its self-defense, including by increasing the defense budget?

- Should the United States resume visits by Cabinet-level officials to Taiwan?

- Should the United States also favor Taiwan's observership (if not membership) in supporting Taiwan's participation in international organizations, such as the World Health Organization (WHO), International Civil Aviation Organization (ICAO), and U.N. Framework Convention on Climate Change (UNFCCC)?

- Should U.S. policy allow or encourage more senior officials from Taiwan to visit and encourage expanded communication with Taiwan's president?

- Should policy allow U.S. flag and general military officers to visit Taiwan?

- How should the United States support transparent, fair, and impartial rule of law, elections, and freedoms in Taiwan, while respecting Taiwan's democracy?

- How should policy press Taiwan to contribute more in weapons nonproliferation, counter-piracy, foreign aid, and other areas of international security?

- What is Taiwan's role in the U.S. comprehensive strategy for rebalancing priorities toward the Asian-Pacific region (so-called "pivot" to the Pacific)?

- Should decision-makers review policy on Taiwan, with the last review in 1994?

- Should the United States press Taiwan to notify the cross-strait Economic Cooperation Framework Agreement (ECFA) of 2010 to the World Trade Organization (WTO) and pay more attention to benefits for U.S. companies?

- How should U.S. policy encourage Taiwan to remove trade and investment barriers?

- With resumption of talks under the 1994 Trade and Investment Framework Agreement (TIFA) after they were in limbo for years due largely to Taiwan's beef restrictions, what should be U.S. priorities to deepen bilateral economic ties?

- Should the United States seek to negotiate a free trade agreement (FTA) or bilateral investment agreement (BIA), and/or support Taiwan's efforts to join multilateral trade negotiations, such as the Trans-Pacific Partnership (TPP)?

- Should Taiwan's growing economic dependence on the PRC be of concern to the United States, and should Taiwan further diversify its economic partners?

Historical Background

Taiwan formally calls itself the Republic of China (ROC), tracing its political lineage to the ROC set up after the revolution in 1911 in China. The ROC does not recognize the PRC founded in Beijing by the Communist Party of China (CPC) in 1949. The PRC claims that the ROC ceased to exist in 1949 and that Taiwan is a province of "one China." (The Qing Empire had incorporated Taiwan as a full province in 1885-1895, when more settlers moved from China to the island.) The PRC and ROC do not recognize each other or two Chinas. The ROC refers to the other side of the strait as the "mainland." The PRC opposes recognition of the ROC and seeks unification of Taiwan with the mainland as a part of "one China," without renouncing the use of force. Taiwan has stated an intention to set aside the dispute over sovereignty. In any case, since 1949, the ROC has governed only on Taiwan, and the PRC based in Beijing has ruled mainland China.

Previously called Formosa, Taiwan never has been ruled by the CPC or as a part of the PRC, and until 1945, had never been ruled by the ROC. In Taiwan after World War II, October 25, 1945, or "Retrocession Day," marked the ROC's claim of "recovering" Formosa from Japan. However, upon Japan's surrender, that was the first time that the ROC's military forces had occupied the island of Formosa. When the Qing Empire ceded in perpetuity Formosa to Japan under the Treaty of Shimonoseki of 1895, the ROC was not yet in existence. Moreover, the colony's people did not have a say in self-determination of their status or identity. The Kuomintang (KMT), or Nationalist Party of China, has contended that the ROC claimed Formosa at Japan's surrender in August 1945, with no country challenging the island's status. The ROC under KMT forces led by Chiang Kai-shek retreated to Taiwan in 1949, when the Communist forces led by Mao Zedong took over mainland China. Taiwan's people have faced social, ethnic, linguistic, and political issues of whether to identify with Taiwan or China, with two major groups of local "Taiwanese" and "Mainlanders" (folks who retreated to Taiwan with the KMT forces and their descendants). The KMT's imposed authoritarian rule and martial law on Taiwan, including a massacre called the "228 Incident" of February 28, 1947, exacerbated difficulties between the groups. President Ma said that over 29,700 victims of the "White Terror" period got compensation by July 2013.

Bipartisan "One China" Policy

One of the first powers to support reforms and the new republic of progressive leaders in early 20th century China, the United States recognized the ROC government from 1913 until the end of 1978.[3] By the early 1970s, the United States looked to switch the diplomatic recognition to the PRC in Beijing while figuring out a framework to maintain the relationship with Taiwan. As a scholar on China and member of the National Security Council staff in 1977-1980 wrote,[4]

> Many factors produced the change in U.S. policy toward China and Taiwan in the 1970s, some tactical, some strategic. The timing of the initial step was unquestionably related to the Vietnam War and the Sino-Soviet dispute. The second and third steps were facilitated by and partly a response to the Soviet expansion. But these were transitory considerations. From a longer-term perspective, America's China policy of the 1950s and 1960s could not be sustained. It was based on American acknowledgment of an absurd claim. Taiwan was not, as it asserted, the government of mainland China. At the same time, China's position was unrealistic. The People's Republic was not the government of Taiwan. In fact, the two governments ruled different parts of Chinese territory, each asserting that it was the rightful authority for all of China, each denying the legitimacy of the other.

The United States has its own "one China" policy (vs. the PRC's "one China" principle) and position on Taiwan's status. Not recognizing the PRC's claim over Taiwan nor Taiwan as a sovereign state, U.S. policy has considered Taiwan's status as unsettled. Since a declaration by President Truman on June 27, 1950, during the Korean War, the United States has supported a future determination of the island's status in a peaceful manner. The United States did not state a stance on the sovereign status of Taiwan in the three U.S.-PRC Joint Communiqués of 1972, 1979, and 1982. The United States simply "acknowledged" the "one China" position of both sides of the Taiwan Strait. Washington has not promised to end arms sales to Taiwan for its self-defense, although the Mutual Defense Treaty of 1954 terminated on December 31, 1979. U.S. policy does not support or oppose Taiwan's independence; U.S. policy takes a neutral position of "non-support" for Taiwan's independence. U.S. policy leaves the Taiwan question to be resolved by the people on both sides of the strait: a "peaceful resolution," with the assent of Taiwan's people in a democratic manner, and without unilateral changes. In short, U.S. policy focuses on the process of resolution of the Taiwan question, not any set outcome.

The United States has maintained a non-diplomatic relationship with Taiwan after recognition of the PRC in Beijing in 1979. The State Department claims an "unofficial" U.S. relationship with Taiwan, despite official contacts that include arms sales. Congress passed a law that did not describe the relationship as official or unofficial. The Taiwan Relations Act (TRA) of 1979, P.L. 96-8, has governed policy in the absence of a diplomatic relationship or a defense treaty. The TRA stipulates the expectation that the future of Taiwan "will be determined" by peaceful means. The TRA specifies that it is policy, inter alia, to consider any non-peaceful means to determine Taiwan's future "a threat" to the peace and security of the Western Pacific and of "grave concern" to the United States; "to provide Taiwan with arms of a defensive character"; and "to maintain the capacity of the United States to resist any resort to force or other forms of coercion" jeopardizing the security, or social or economic system of Taiwan's people. The TRA provides a congressional

---

[3] Jonathan Spence, *The Search for Modern China* (New York: W. W. Norton & Company, 1990).

[4] Michel Oksenberg, "Taiwan, Tibet, and Hong Kong in Sino-American Relations," in *Living with China*, edited by Ezra Vogel (New York: W. W. Norton & Company, 1997).

role in determining security assistance "necessary to enable Taiwan to maintain a sufficient self-defense capability." The TRA set up the American Institute in Taiwan (AIT) to carry out the day-to-day matters of the relationship to sustain U.S. interests after the de-recognition of the ROC. Since 1979, the TRA has had bipartisan support in guiding policy with a firm foundation and flexible framework for the maintenance of the relationship with Taiwan.

In addition to the three Joint communiqués and the TRA, there is a fifth key statement that guides U.S. policy on Taiwan. President Reagan offered "Six Assurances" to Taipei on July 14, 1982, that in negotiating the third Joint Communiqué with the PRC, the United States: (1) has not agreed to set a date for ending arms sales to Taiwan; (2) has not agreed to hold prior consultations with the PRC on arms sales to Taiwan; (3) will not play any mediation role between Taipei and Beijing; (4) has not agreed to revise the Taiwan Relations Act; (5) has not altered its position regarding sovereignty over Taiwan; and (6) will not exert pressure on Taiwan to negotiate with the PRC. (Also see CRS Report RL30341, *China/Taiwan: Evolution of the "One China" Policy— Key Statements from Washington, Beijing, and Taipei,* by Shirley A. Kan.)

Democratic Politics

Since those years when the United States dealt with the KMT authoritarian government in Taipei, the relationship has grown both more robust and more complex with Taiwan's democratization and shared values about freedom. The United States supported Taiwan's political liberalization from an authoritarian dictatorship to a dynamic democracy. Democratization and electoral politics have allowed the people a greater say in Taiwan's identity (as part of China or a separate entity). In 1986, the KMT did not crack down against the formation of Taiwan's second major party, the Democratic Progressive Party (DPP), which has leaned toward Taiwan's independence. The KMT then lifted Martial Law in 1987. In 1999, the DPP passed a Resolution on Taiwan's Future. It declared, *inter alia*, that after the elections for the national legislature in 1992, direct presidential election in 1996, and constitutional reform to abolish the provincial government, Taiwan became a democratic and independent country. The Resolution stated that Taiwan is not a part of the PRC and that Taiwan's formal national title is "Republic of China." This situation is the "status quo."

At times, the PRC has reacted unfavorably to Taiwan's democratic politics and implications for sovereignty, particularly since its first democratic, direct presidential election in March 1996. The PRC's People's Liberation Army (PLA) "test-fired" missiles into sea areas close to Taiwan, which provoked the Taiwan Strait Crisis of 1995-1996. President Clinton deployed two aircraft carrier battle groups near Taiwan in March 1996. The PRC threatened Taiwan after President Lee Teng-hui characterized the cross-strait relationship as "special state-to-state ties" on July 9, 1999. On March 18, 2000, Chen Shui-bian of the DPP won the presidential election. Chen's DPP administration brought Taiwan's first democratic transfer of power from one party to another, after 55 years of KMT rule. In recognition of Taiwan's democracy, President Clinton declared in 2000 another condition that the resolution of the Taiwan question must be peaceful as well as with the "assent" of Taiwan's people. In 2003, President Bush expressed "opposition" to any unilateral decision to change the "status quo." On the TRA's 25th anniversary, Representative James Leach said at a hearing of the House International Relations Committee on April 21, 2004, that Taiwan has the unique situation in which it can have *de facto* self-determination only if it does not attempt to be recognized with *de jure* sovereignty. He urged Taiwan's people to recognize that they have greater security in "political ambiguity."

Cross-strait tension rose again when the PRC accused President Chen (2000-2008) of promoting Taiwan's *de jure* independence (e.g., with a referendum on Taiwan's membership in the U.N.

during the presidential election on March 22, 2008). While opposing such referendums, President Bush positioned two aircraft carriers near Taiwan, as the largely symbolic referendums were still targets of the PRC's belligerent condemnation. The referendums failed to be valid. The victory of the KMT's Ma Ying-jeou ushered in Taiwan's second democratic transfer of power from one party to another. Bush congratulated Taiwan as a "beacon of democracy." Some have stressed Taiwan as a model democracy in a Chinese cultural context. (Also see CRS Report RL34441, *Security Implications of Taiwan's Presidential Election of March 2008*, by Shirley Kan.)

The KMT's March 2008 presidential victory was preceded on January 12, 2008, by a sweeping victory in which it swamped the DPP in elections for the Legislative Yuan (LY). Having won the presidency as well in March, the KMT assumed solid control of the government in May 2008. The 2008 legislative elections were the first held under new electoral rules adopted in 2005 under an amendment to Taiwan's constitution. The rules cut in half the size of the LY to 113 members from its former size of 225 and increased the term of office from three years to four years. The rules also instituted a new single-member district system employing two ballots for voters, similar to systems used in Germany and Japan: one to be cast for a candidate and one to be cast for a political party. As demonstrated by the electoral results, the new system favored larger, well-organized parties and put smaller parties at a disadvantage. Two smaller opposition parties have been the People's First Party (PFP), initially allied with the KMT as "Blue" parties, and the Taiwan Solidarity Union (TSU), siding with the DPP as "Green" parties. Compared to the KMT, the DPP and TSU have been more Taiwan-centric in their perspectives and wary of the PRC.

Major Developments in Cross-Strait Engagement

Ties or tension across the Taiwan Strait affect international security (with potential U.S. intervention), the U.S.-Taiwan relationship, and U.S.-PRC cooperation. Congressional oversight has been concerned with support for U.S. interests, particularly respect for Taiwan's democracy. Since their first direct talks in 1992, Taiwan and the PRC have negotiated through quasi-official organizations: the **Strait Exchange Foundation (SEF)** in Taipei and the **Association for Relations Across the Taiwan Strait (ARATS)** in Beijing. In discussing practical issues in initial contact, the two sides agreed to disagree on the meaning of "one China" with the verbal formula of "One China, Different Interpretations." To Taipei, "China" is the ROC. To Beijing, "China" is the PRC. However, years later, the CPC in Beijing and KMT in Taipei shifted to contend that they reached a "1992 Consensus." The DPP has disputed that there was a "consensus" and has argued that any understanding was reached between two political parties without a democratic mandate.

Resumed Dialogue and Reduced Tension

In the two months between his election and his inauguration on May 20, 2008, President Ma spoke of his intentions to begin normalizing cross-strait ties in a "cross-strait common market," to establish direct air links with the PRC, and to ease other restrictions on cross-strait contacts. In his inaugural address, President Ma announced his "Three Noes": "no unification, no independence, and no use of force" to maintain the "status quo" and set aside the sovereignty dispute. He called for a "diplomatic truce" with the PRC and pledged to stop using "dollar diplomacy" in a zero-sum game to win or preserve diplomatic recognition around the world.[5] After his inauguration,

---

[5] "Dollar diplomacy" (or "checkbook diplomacy") refers to both Taiwan and the PRC competing for diplomatic
(continued...)

President Ma moved to improve cross-strait engagement, building on foundations laid by the previous President Chen.[6] KMT Chairman Wu Poh-hsiung met with CPC General Secretary Hu Jintao on May 28, 2008, the highest-level encounter between the two governments after 1949.[7]

Along with Washington's actions to maintain the relationship with Taipei, it has pursued closer engagement and reduced tension across the Taiwan Strait. Although the PRC objects to U.S. security assistance to Taiwan as harming cross-strait "peaceful development," economic integration and other engagement between Taiwan and the PRC have intensified. Taipei contends that U.S. support provides it with confidence and strength to engage with Beijing.

Cross-Strait Agreements

In June 2008, KMT President Ma Ying-jeou and the PRC leadership resumed the cross-strait dialogue (after a decade) and pursued closer engagement, beyond seeking détente. President Ma announced a priority of economic talks over political negotiations with Beijing. Taiwan's reality involved the PRC as Taiwan's largest trading partner by 2003 and as many as 2 million of its citizens already working and living on the mainland by 2008. By the end of 2009, Taiwan's companies had invested about $150 billion in over 77,000 projects in the past 20 years there.[8]

Since 2008, Taiwan has announced nine rounds of SEF-ARATS talks along with the conclusion of 19 cross-strait primarily economic agreements. Those agreements included the Economic Cooperation Framework Agreement (ECFA) to lower tariffs or relax access for 539 products and services from Taiwan. Though politically controversial, President Ma promoted the ECFA amid the opposition DPP's protests and negotiated it within months, from January 2010 until it was signed in June 2010. A range of government officials and their counterparts developed routine contacts across the strait, including through phone calls. In May 2010, the two sides opened the first quasi-official agencies (as tourism offices) in Beijing and Taipei. Two dramatic changes cited by Taiwan's people and foreign businesspeople have been direct flights across the strait and an increase in tourists from the mainland. From mid-2008, when Taiwan allowed PRC tour groups, until the end of 2011, 3 million PRC tourists visited Taiwan.[9] In June 2011, Taiwan announced deals that allowed individual mainland tourists and increased direct flights from 370 to 560 a week. In 2013, weekly passenger flights totaled 616 and cargo flights totaled 56. Visits by PRC travelers (including those from Hong Kong and Macau) totaled 3.6 million in 2012, accounting for about half of all visits. Taiwan's dependence on PRC travelers increased. In August 2013, Taiwan said that passenger flights would further increase to 670 a week.

Starting in 2009, Taiwan looked to conclude an agreement on investment protection for Taiwan's business people, but negotiations were difficult over issues that involved dispute resolution (whether to have an international mechanism). After postponing an investment protection

---

(...continued)

relations by promising to and investing huge sums in countries that may be wavering in their diplomatic allegiances.

[6] Among other initiatives during the Chen Administration, in January 2005, Taiwan and the PRC launched the first non-stop holiday direct charter flights flown in 55 years across the strait. These were expanded in 2006 with an agreement to allow up to 168 direct annual round-trip charter passenger flights between the PRC and Taiwan.

[7] On April 29, 2005, when the KMT was out of power, KMT Chairman Lien Chan met with CPC General Secretary Hu Jintao, the first time the leaders of the KMT and CPC had met since World War II.

[8] Kathrin Hille, "Straitened Times," *Financial Times*, March 26, 2008; *CNA*, Taipei, December 23, 2009.

[9] *Central News Agency*, Taipei, January 4, 2012.

agreement expected in June 2012, the two sides announced in August two agreements on investment protection (including some allowance for arbitration) and customs cooperation. At the 9th round of talks on June 21, 2013, the two sides signed the 19th agreement (on trade in services).

Continuing Challenges

Despite the announcements of those agreements, the two sides did not sign an expected agreement on taxation in 2009, in a dispute over the PRC's proposal to tax income from stock trading. At the 7th round in October 2011, the two sides also announced a "consensus" (not agreement) on industrial cooperation. After failing to reach an agreement between banking regulators in April 2011, the two sides announced a "consensus" in November. Still, the Taiwan side believed it pragmatically negotiated benefits for its banks. Also, at the end of August 2012, Taiwan and the PRC signed a memorandum of understanding (MOU) on currency clearing.

Taiwan continues to face challenges in protecting its citizens from detentions in the PRC (including secret detentions in PRC "black jails"). From June 18, 2012, just before the investment protection agreement was expected, until August 11, the PRC's Ministry of State Security (MSS) detained Chung Ting-pang (Bruce Chung), a visitor from Taiwan, for allegedly sabotaging national and public security in activities associated with Falun Gong (a banned group in the PRC). Representative Dana Rohrabacher wrote a letter on July 10 to urge President Ma to speak out strongly against Chung's detention. (Later, on December 18, Chung testified at a hearing chaired by Representative Christopher Smith and Senator Sherrod Brown of the Congressional-Executive Commission on China (CECC). Chung discussed interrogations about his activities and about other Falun Gong practitioners in Taiwan. He also commented that the Ma Administration was relatively passive in securing his release.) Taiwan said it got a separate "consensus" in August on protecting the safety of Taiwan's business people. However, questions remained about protections for visitors not doing business, not detained by the police but the MSS, held in security-related cases, detained in secret, and denied prompt, private, and repeated visits by relatives, officials, and lawyers (not just notifications of detentions to relatives). Other questions concerned Taiwan's enforcement of PRC promises and securing the release of other detained citizens. New York University's (NYU's) legal scholar, Jerome Cohen, offered a critique.[10]

The pace has slowed in signing cross-strait agreements since 2008. The initial pace of signing multiple agreements a year was not sustained. While there were two rounds of talks in each year of 2008, 2009, and 2010, the 7th round took place in 2011, the 8th in 2012, and the 9th in 2013. Though the agreement to expand trade in services was expected to be signed at the 9th round of talks in June 2013, some legislators and groups raised concerns that Taiwan's Mainland Affairs Council (MAC) did not fully brief the LY and allow time for debate about the agreement, that the talks lacked transparency, that the MAC did not adequately consult in advance with the many affected industries, and that the MAC did not present an assessment of positive and negative impacts or national security implications. Both KMT and DPP legislators called for the LY's detailed review of the agreement (not just its report to the LY). After the agreement was signed, President Ma argued on June 28 that it would help in Taiwan's economic liberalization, involve Taiwan in regional trade talks, and advance cross-strait ties.[11] Ma asks for the LY's approval.

---

[10] Jerome Cohen and Yu-Jie Chen, "For Taiwanese, the Mainland Remains a Dangerous Place," *South China Morning Post*, Hong Kong, September 5, 2012; Author's interview with Bruce Chung, December 2012.

[11] *Central News Agency*, May 27, June 14, June 19, June 25, June 28; *Taipei Times*, May 28, June 22, June 26, 2013.

The United States has welcomed the reduction in tension brought by economic and people-to-people engagement across the Taiwan Strait. Aside from increased stability and direct flights, however, it has been less clear how the agreements, especially ECFA, have benefitted U.S. and other foreign firms. Deputy Assistant Secretary of State David Shear said in July 2010 that "if ECFA is to be a truly successful arrangement, firms from the United States and other countries must also be able to benefit." Taiwan announced that ECFA entered into force on September 12, 2010. However, some have concerns that Taiwan has not notified ECFA to the WTO, as required of its members. Taiwan's officials have claimed that there was a notification, but Taiwan made only an early announcement. Moreover, even as Taipei quickly negotiated ECFA with Beijing from January to June 2010, Taipei did not devote a similar level of attention to resolving the dispute with Washington over beef (see discussion below). Further, in mid-2011, the American Chamber of Commerce (AmCham) in Taipei noted that 41.7% of Taiwan's exports went to the PRC (including Hong Kong) and warned Taiwan against the risks of over-reliance on one market. AmCham urged Taiwan to pursue balanced relationships that include stronger ties with other countries, particularly the United States as part of a national security agenda. When asked in 2013 about the effect of ECFA on their business, 37% of AmCham's members in Taiwan which answered its survey said that the effect was neutral, 44% saw some positive effect, 5% saw very positive effect, 10% did not know, and the remaining 4% reported some or very negative effect.[12]

In addition, some observers pointed out that Taiwan could increase substantive visits to the United States by its Minister of Economic Affairs. Cross-strait flights raised an issue of whether they have helped or harmed U.S. and other foreign airlines, aside from Taiwan and PRC airlines. In September 2012, AmCham published an article, lamenting that the shipping links set up across the strait in 2008 have done little to help Taiwan realize its aspiration of becoming a shipping hub, since the arrangement excluded foreign carriers from cross-strait shipping.

Questions also have arisen about Taiwan's reviews of technology transfers to the PRC and any national security implications of increasing PRC investments in Taiwan, including how Taiwan's review of PRC investments compares with the U.S. security review by the Committee on Foreign Investment in the United States (CFIUS) and how Taiwan's Ministry of Economic Affairs (MOEA) is cooperating with the PRC's Ministry of Industry and Information Technology (MIIT).[13] The MIIT is part of the PRC's defense industrial structure. In November 2013, as President Ma sought the LY's approval of the cross-strait agreement on trade in services signed in June, the Investment Commission of the Ministry of Economic Affairs (MOEA) announced stricter rules for investments by PRC companies in Taiwan that threaten security or are sensitive.

Taiwan has tried to use ECFA as a springboard for bilateral economic agreements. Taiwan also has faced challenges in joining multilateral trade talks (like the TPP), although it has the option of unilateral liberalization of trade and investment rules. On July 10, 2013, Taiwan and New Zealand signed a bilateral agreement. Taiwan touted the value of the agreement, because New Zealand is one of the countries in the TPP.[14] Taiwan later signed the Agreement between Singapore and Taiwan on Economic Partnership (ASTEP) on November 7.

---

[12] AmCham Taipei, "Business Climate Survey," *Taiwan Business Topics*, February 2013.

[13] In Taipei in August 2013, a vice minister of Taiwan's MOEA and a vice minister of the PRC's MIIT reportedly attended the "2013 Conference on Cross-Strait High-Tech Industrial Investment, Cooperation, and Procurement."

[14] The Agreement between New Zealand and the Separate Customs Territory of Taiwan, Penghu, Kinmen, and Matsu on Economic Cooperation (ANZTEC). Later in July 2013, Japan joined the TPP talks as the 12th member, along with Australia, Brunei, Canada, Chile, Malaysia, Mexico, New Zealand, Peru, Singapore, the United States, and Vietnam.

Further, despite the cross-strait warming trend, concerns remain about the PLA's challenges to Taiwan. At a hearing on Taiwan held by the House Foreign Affairs Committee on October 4, 2011, Acting Assistant Secretary of Defense Peter Lavoy expressed the U.S. concern that a Taiwan that is vulnerable, isolated, and under threat would not be in a position to discuss its future with the mainland and might invite the very aggression U.S. policy seeks to deter. He warned that if the PLA were to attack, it would be able to rapidly degrade Taiwan's ability to resist. Lavoy testified that the Defense Department's report to Congress on Taiwan's air power concluded that Taiwan's defense cannot match the PLA one-for-one. He reiterated the Pentagon's view that Taiwan needs innovative and asymmetric approaches, not simply limited numbers of advanced weapons systems.

On March 5, 2013, the Commander of the Pacific Command (PACOM), Admiral Samuel Locklear, testified to the House Armed Services Committee that the cross-strait relationship is stable and tensions are at historic lows due to economic integration and people-to-people contact. However, he warned that the PLA continues to maintain a robust military buildup against Taiwan that contradicts the PRC's stated "peaceful development" of ties with Taiwan. He reported that many of the PLA's developments appeared to be intended for use in a possible conflict with Taiwan (including ballistic and cruise missiles, patrol boats, mines, electronic warfare, and cyber threats). Director of National Intelligence (DNI) James Clapper testified to the Senate Intelligence Committee on March 12 that the cross-strait relationship remained calm but the military and economic balance will keep shifting in China's favor.

In May 2013, the Defense Secretary reported to Congress that China has continued its military modernization with potential conflict in the Taiwan Strait (with possible U.S. intervention) as the principal focus and primary driver. Despite the reduction of cross-strait tension since 2008, the PLA's disposition opposite Taiwan has not changed significantly, and the PLA could attempt to coerce or invade Taiwan. The worrisome trend in the Taiwan Strait has seen the PLA's more sophisticated capabilities improving against Taiwan's eroding defensive advantages, even while Taiwan's military spending has dropped to about 2% of GDP (below President Ma's promise of 3% of GDP). The PLA's advanced capabilities include over 1,100 short-range ballistic missiles, as well as attack submarines and ships, fighters, and long-range surface-to-air missiles.[15]

Observers might watch to see whether President Ma ensures greater transparency about cross-strait negotiations and agreements for Taiwan domestically, the United States and other countries, and international groups. Since 2005, the CPC and KMT have proposed a "peace agreement" and military confidence building measures (CBMs). In campaigning for re-election in October 2011, Ma raised the controversial idea of a cross-strait peace accord. Beijing took the results of Taiwan's elections in January 2012 as validation of the "peaceful development" approach. On that basis, Beijing could continue patient engagement focused first on economics and refrain from pressuring Ma, given cross-party criticism of his leadership and his low approval ratings.

Further into Ma's second term, however, Beijing could increase pressure on Taiwan, in preparing for if not pressing for political and military negotiations. In March 2012, two months before Ma's second inaugural address, the CPC Taiwan Affairs Office (TAO) in Beijing called for a new phase of consolidating political mutual trust, negotiating economic benefits for both sides (not just for Taiwan), and shaping Taiwan's cultural understanding of the "national identity" of "one China"

---

[15] Secretary of Defense, "Annual Report to Congress: Military and Security Developments Involving the People's Republic of China, 2013," May 6, 2013.

(including "cleaning up" harmful thoughts about "Taiwan independence"). Moreover, KMT Honorary Chairman Wu Poh-hsiung met in Beijing with CPC General-Secretary Hu Jintao, who called for actions to build "political trust" with the insistence that "the mainland and Taiwan belong to one China." On his part, the KMT's Wu stressed the concept of "one country, two areas." The opposition DPP criticized the "one country, two areas" formula, stressing that Taiwan is a sovereign country and does not belong to the PRC. A month before Ma's inaugural address, TAO Director Wang Yi visited Washington in April, where he met with Deputy Secretary of State William Burns. Wang indicated Beijing's expectation of future political talks with Taipei.[16]

In his second inaugural address on May 20, 2012, President Ma did not repeat either of those phrases. Ma apparently assured Beijing about his cross-strait policy but asserted limits in accommodating on sovereignty. While Ma upheld the "1992 Consensus" (explicitly defined as "One China, Different Interpretations"), he more explicitly and formally added that "one ROC, two areas" defines the two sides of the Taiwan Strait. Ma asserted that the two sides practice "mutual non-recognition of sovereignty and mutual non-denial of governing authority," because the ROC's sovereignty covers Taiwan and the mainland, but the ROC governs only the islands of Taiwan, Penghu, Kinmen, and Matsu. However, Ma reiterated the principle in the first inaugural address of maintaining the "status quo" of what he called "no unification, no independence, and no use of force." Further, Ma seemed to agree with Beijing on cultural cooperation, saying that civic groups could expand exchanges across the strait based on what he called common Chinese ethnicity, ancestry, bloodline, history, culture, and founding father (Sun Yat-sen). Still, he also stressed democracy, human rights, rule of law, and civil society. While Ma noted that national security is the key to the ROC's "survival," he articulated an approach that relied on cross-strait engagement, diplomacy for international space, and defense. On his defense policy, Ma did not explicitly cite the PLA as the threat but called for continued U.S. arms sales in order to sustain the cross-strait engagement. While the English version of his speech called for a "strong national defense" to deter external threats, the original text in Chinese referred to the "national defense forces." At a conference four days later, President Ma invoked the model of West Germany and East Germany on a distinction between sovereignty and governing authority.

It was unclear if Ma's message was coordinated as part of parallel statements that involved control of Wu's meeting with Hu, a counter to Hu's position, or a compromise. On May 30, when asked about Ma's "One ROC, Two Areas" formulation, the CPC TAO responded that it was not surprising and was consistent with the view that both sides of the strait belong to one China (rather than a "state-to-state relationship") and beneficial to the peaceful development of the cross-strait ties. However, the TAO rejected use of the model of the two Germanys.

Beijing's patience could be tested further by the sustained separate identity in Taiwan. Despite the pronouncements of a "one China" by leaders in Taipei and Beijing and closer cross-strait ties, Taiwan's people retain a strong Taiwan-centric identity after over a century of mostly separation from mainland China. Still, Taiwan's people pragmatically have pursued prosperity, security, and their democratic way of life and self-governance. Moderate voters generally have supported economic ties to the PRC amid political separation. In August 2012, only 0.9% of those surveyed in Taiwan wished for cross-strait unification as soon as possible, while 84% desired the status quo (at least indefinitely or with a later decision on unification or independence), 7% called for independence as soon as possible, and the remaining 8% voiced no opinion. The results showed even weaker support for urgent unification, compared with results back in August 2008 (shortly

---

[16] TAO, Beijing, March 15; *Xinhua*, Beijing, and *CNA*, Taipei, March 22; *Taipei Times*, April 14, 2012.

after Ma became president), when 1.5% desired unification as soon as possible, 83% opted for the status quo, 9% called for independence as soon as possible, and 7% voiced no opinion.[17]

At the 18th National Congress of the CPC in Beijing in November 2012, outgoing CPC General Secretary Hu Jintao delivered a report that was drafted by a group led by incoming CPC General Secretary Xi Jinping. The report called for strengthening political, economic, cultural, and social cross-strait ties to achieve eventual "peaceful reunification." While stressing political ties first and without new initiatives, the report indicated that top-level authoritative policy would continue to call for the "1992 Consensus," military CBMs, and a peace agreement.

On his part, Taiwan President Ma said in his New Year day address for 2013 that he will cooperate with Xi Jinping on the basis of the "1992 Consensus," but Ma clarified that each side of the strait retains its own interpretation of what "one China" means. Ma said that his policy would seek to expand all aspects of cross-strait ties while stressing economic and people-to-people ties. Ma said that Taiwan will seek to loosen further the restrictions on investments, students, and individual travelers from the mainland, including through amendment of the "Act Governing Relations between the People of the Taiwan Area and the Mainland Area." Moving on to a political matter, Ma said that the two sides would establish reciprocal, representative offices.

In addition, President Ma has to deal with a political propensity in his own party to move even closer to the PRC. In February 2013, KMT Honorary Chairman Lien Chan met in Beijing with Xi Jinping. Furthermore, Lien visited the Beijing Aerospace Control Center, though the PLA controls the PRC's space program. Ma's office stressed that he did not give Lien any message to convey.

Starting in April 2013, negotiations for setting up the representative offices reportedly raised issues (in the KMT and opposition parties) about sovereignty and national flags, legal immunity and inviolability, equal and reciprocal rights, official visits to (not just notifications of) detained citizens (including Taiwan's intelligence agents in China), issuance of travel permits (visas), non-interference in Taiwan's elections, security, and political talks. Before Taiwan completed talks over the representative offices, the Ma Administration asked the LY to pass the legal authority in June, but KMT, DPP, PFP, and TSU lawmakers balked at granting a "blank check." According to Taiwan officials, Taiwan has about 1,500 citizens who were detained or imprisoned in the PRC.

In June, President and KMT Chairman Ma again sent KMT Honorary Chairman Wu Poh-hsiung to Beijing to meet with CPC General-Secretary Xi Jinping and maintain momentum in cross-strait engagement. After adding the phrase of "one country, two areas" the previous year, Wu added this time that the ties are under the "one China framework," another phrase different from the vague "1992 Consensus." Wu conveyed Ma's message that representative offices would not be diplomatic offices since cross-strait ties are not "state-to-state" under the ROC's constitution. Wu also sought support for Taiwan's participation in international organizations and economic talks. The DPP criticized the KMT's use of "one China framework" as harming Taiwan's sovereignty. The KMT's use of "one China framework" seemed to complicate efforts for forging a domestic consensus. The nuanced shift came as the DPP shifted to be willing to discuss the "1992 Consensus." In July, the DPP's China Affairs Committee talked about the "1992 Consensus." The next month, Kaohsiung Mayor Chen Chu visited the PRC for a second time, though she did not represent the DPP. The PRC's TAO Director Zhang Zhijun met with Chen in Tianjin.

---

[17] Surveys conducted by the Election Study Center at the National Chengchi University in Taipei, Taiwan.

In October 2013, CPC General Secretary Xi Jinping seemed to raise pressure on Ma Ying-jeou to agree to political talks. At the Asia-Pacific Economic Cooperation (APEC) leaders' summit in Bali, Indonesia, Xi told Ma's representative, former vice president Vincent Siew, that the long-term political differences across the strait should be resolved gradually and that they should not be passed from one generation to another. Siew sought Xi's support for cross-strait economic cooperation and "joint participation" in regional economic integration. In Bali, Taiwan's MAC Minister Wang Yu-chi met with the PRC's TAO Director Zhang Zhijun for the first time. In an interview with the *Washington Post* on October 24, Ma defended Taiwan's approach and denied avoiding political issues. He said that Taiwan deals with political issues when the time is ripe.

Issues in U.S. Policy on Taiwan

Overview

The Administration and Congress have considered various options to strengthen the relationship with Taiwan. One issue has been whether to resume Cabinet-level visits, perhaps by the Secretaries of Homeland Security, Agriculture, Veteran Affairs, Commerce, or Energy, or the U.S. Trade Representative (USTR). Such officials visited Taiwan in 1992, 1994, 1996, 1998, and 2000.

In 2011, Taiwan's political campaigning constrained U.S. influence on some policy priorities, particularly opening Taiwan's market to U.S. beef. There was some expectation that after the elections in January 2012, Taiwan would pay greater attention to the relationship with the United States. Both Washington and Taipei describe the relationship as generally a positive one of an economic and security partnership based on shared values. On the U.S. side, the Legislative and Executive Branches took actions to strengthen the relationship. On September 14, 2011, Representative Ileana Ros-Lehtinen, chair of the House Foreign Affairs Committee, introduced the Taiwan Policy Act (H.R. 2918) to enhance ties with Taiwan. The House Foreign Affairs Committee held hearings on "Why Taiwan Matters" on June 16 and October 4, 2011.

In September 2011, the Obama Administration met with visiting delegations from Taiwan's presidential candidates, led by DPP candidate Tsai Ing-wen and a key advisor in KMT President Ma's campaign (King Pu-tsung). There was a congressional reception for Tsai. However, the Administration promptly gave negative remarks to the *Financial Times*, saying that Tsai raised doubts about continuing cross-strait "stability," despite professing U.S. neutrality in Taiwan's democratic elections. The Administration then notified Congress on September 21 of three major arms sales programs with a total value of $5.9 billion, including upgrades for Taiwan's existing F-16A/B fighters. The Administration also increased senior visits to Taiwan, sending Assistant Secretary of Commerce Suresh Kumar in September and then U.S. Agency for International Development (USAID) Administrator Rajiv Shah and Deputy Secretary of Energy Dan Poneman in December 2011. After not mentioning Taiwan in an article in *Foreign Policy* on "America's Pacific Century" in October 2011, Secretary of State Hillary Clinton gave a speech on the same subject the next month and added that the United States has a strong relationship with Taiwan as an "important security and economic partner." On December 22, the State Department nominated Taiwan as a candidate for the Visa Waiver Program (VWP), and Taiwan's Foreign Ministry touted the long-awaited announcement as a "Christmas gift" in appreciation to the Ma Administration.

The Obama Administration has argued that its efforts to intensify and expand cooperative engagement with the PRC in Beijing have not been at the expense of a stronger relationship with

Taiwan. Washington officials contend that they have pursued parallel relationships with Beijing and Taipei. Nonetheless, policy issues have included whether the Administration actually has ambitious objectives to achieve in the relationship with Taipei, has timed arms sales and certain other actions out of concern about the relationship with Beijing, strengthened ties with Taiwan in the months before the elections in January 2012 to favor President Ma, should resume U.S. Cabinet-level visits, has been effective in encouraging Taiwan to raise the priority of defense, or has included Taiwan in the strategy to "rebalance" U.S. priorities to the Asia-Pacific.

On Taiwan's side, President Ma "transited" in the United States, where he sometimes met with Members of Congress and joined public activities: in Los Angeles, Austin, and San Francisco on his way to and from Paraguay and the Dominican Republic in 2008; in San Francisco and Honolulu on his way to and from Panama and Nicaragua in 2009; in San Francisco and Los Angeles on his way to and from Honduras and the Dominican Republic in 2010; and in New York and Los Angeles on his way to and from Paraguay, Haiti, Saint Kitts and Nevis, Saint Lucia, and Saint Vincent and the Grenadines in August 2013. President Ma asserted that he rebuilt U.S.-Taiwan trust by not raising cross-strait tension. Particularly with the sensitive political season over in January 2012, President Ma said he placed priority on the relationship with the United States. However, some observers stressed that Taiwan needed to restore some trust lost in the relationship and reciprocate U.S. efforts to strengthen it. Although President Ma has served also as the Chairman of the ruling KMT, he faced a challenge (some called a "crisis") for years to lead his administration and party to resolve the disputes over U.S. beef and pork.

On the occasion of President Ma's second inauguration on May 20, 2012, Representative Ros-Lehtinen led a congressional delegation to visit Taiwan. In meetings with the Codel and the delegation led by former White House chief of staff William Daley that represented the Obama Administration, President Ma said that Taiwan seeks to join the TPP (though in eight years).

On the strategic rebalancing toward the Pacific region, issues have concerned whether U.S. strategy considers Taiwan's security role narrowly in the Taiwan Strait or more broadly in the Pacific, and what Taiwan has contributed. After not mentioning Taiwan in an article on a U.S. "pivot" to the Pacific in *Foreign Policy* on "America's Pacific Century" in October 2011, Secretary of State Clinton gave a speech on the same subject the next month in Honolulu and added that the United States has a strong relationship with Taiwan as an "important security and economic partner." At the start of 2012, President Obama and Defense Secretary Leon Panetta issued new Defense Strategic Guidance on how to maintain U.S. military superiority in the face of budget cuts and to "rebalance" priorities, posture, and presence to stress more attention to Asia as well as the Middle East. An issue arose about Taiwan's role in the U.S. comprehensive strategy of rebalancing more diplomatic, defense, and economic attention to Asia. At a conference of defense ministers in Singapore in June 2012, Defense Secretary Panetta discussed the strategic refocus to Asia and mentioned Taiwan by saying that the United States strongly supports the efforts of both the PRC and Taiwan to improve the cross-strait relationship. He added that "we have an enduring interest in peace and stability across the Taiwan Strait." Taiwan's Deputy Defense Minister Andrew Yang said he discussed Taiwan's role in the rebalancing strategy with U.S. officials in August and with Deputy Secretary of Defense Ashton Carter on October 2, 2012.[18] Meanwhile, Assistant Secretary of State for Economic and Business Affairs Jose

---

[18] Defense Department, Remarks by Secretary Panetta at the Shangri-La Dialogue in Singapore, June 2, 2012; Author's consultation, August 2012; Yang's interview with *Defense News*, published on November 12, 2012.

Fernandez visited Taipei in August 2012. He delivered a speech that discussed economic exchanges with Taiwan in the context of the strategic rebalancing toward Asia.

For years, the United States and Taiwan sought to resume trade talks under the Trade and Investment Framework Agreement (TIFA), or TIFA talks. However, Taiwan's restrictions on U.S. beef raised concerns. TIFA talks resumed in March 2013, for the first time since July 2007. Since then, Chairmen Ed Royce and Robert Menendez of the House Foreign Affairs and Senate Foreign Relations Committees, and other Members, have supported a bilateral investment agreement (BIA). Saying that he was "optimistic" about the U.S.-Taiwan relationship, Deputy Assistant Secretary of State Kin Moy also noted a potential BIA in his speech on October 3. He said that "Taiwan remains a close partner with whom we engage in a full range of substantive interactions, including trade negotiations, scientific and technological cooperation, environmental protection, academic and cultural exchanges, delegation visits, and security cooperation."[19]

International Security

The United States has watched Taiwan's contribution to international development and security. The United States could work with Taiwan to increase cooperation in international security. Taiwan could boost its defense and foreign aid spending, fight cyber threats, and improve counter-espionage amid cases in Taiwan of alleged spying for Beijing. Taiwan has the option to increase military or civilian missions in humanitarian assistance and disaster relief (HA/DR).

In response to Haiti's devastating earthquake in January 2010, Taiwan's air force delivered relief supplies on a C-130 transport plane, which received approval for refueling and repair at U.S. bases. Taiwan, as the ROC, has a diplomatic relationship with Haiti. After Japan's catastrophic earthquake, tsunami, and nuclear disaster in March 2011, President Ma led Taiwan to be the largest donor of official and private aid, including $3.5 million from the government, though Taiwan did not offer military and coast guard assistance to Japan. Although the USAID Administrator's visit in 2011 highlighted Taiwan's role as an aid donor, Taiwan's foreign assistance amounted to US$380 million in 2010 and in 2011, accounting for 0.1% of gross national income (compared to the international average of 0.5%). On September 25, 2012, in Taipei, President Ma spoke at a conference on international aid, touting Taiwan's development aid but promising to maintain the aid budget (not to raise it). However, Taiwan's 2013 foreign aid budget reportedly dropped by almost 20% (to about US$366 million). After Typhoon Haiyan devastated the Philippines on November 8, 2013, Taiwan donated $200,000 in official aid and used Air Force C-130 transport aircraft to deliver private charitable and official supplies.

The United States has gained counterterrorism cooperation at ports through Taiwan's agreements in 2005 and 2006 to participate in the Container Security Initiative (CSI) (to screen and inspect cargo before shipping to U.S. ports) and the Megaports Initiative (to detect and interdict nuclear and other radioactive materials in cargo). The U.S. Department of Energy and Taiwan's Ministry of Finance and Directorate of Customs completed the installation of radiation detection equipment at the southern port of Kaohsiung in February 2011. Visiting Taipei in December 2011, Deputy Secretary of Energy Poneman personally applauded the milestone reached after five years of effort. He remarked that Taiwan has worked with the U.S. National Nuclear Security Administration (NNSA) to strengthen nuclear security at ports to detect nuclear smuggling.

---

[19] Kin Moy, "Trends in the U.S.-Taiwan Relationship," Carnegie Endowment for International Peace, October 3, 2013.

The United States also has sought Taiwan's cooperation in nuclear and missile nonproliferation efforts especially concerning Iran and North Korea, reportedly involving Taiwan's companies. For example, in March 2009, the Shanghai-based Roc-Master Manufacture and Supply Company reportedly ordered 108 pressure gauges that could be used in centrifuges to enrich uranium for transfer to Iran from an agent in Taiwan (Heli-Ocean Technology Company) for Inficon Holding, the manufacturer in Switzerland. In July 2010, Taiwan reportedly raided Ho Li Enterprises which received orders since March 2007 from Dandong Fang Lian Trading Company in Dandong, PRC, which was allegedly associated with North Korea's military, for two dual-use, high-technology machine tools that ended up in North Korea earlier in 2010. In August 2012, the United States reportedly asked a Taiwan shipping company not to allow its ship to transfer suspected weapons-related cargo in Malaysia that North Korea shipped via China bound for Burma (Myanmar). Japan then seized the cargo. In October 2012, a U.S. court sentenced a Taiwan woman to two years in prison for using her companies in Taiwan to procure embargoed technology for Iran.[20] In May 2013, an U.S. Attorney's Office in Illinois announced the arrests in Estonia and the United States of two citizens of Taiwan, Alex Tsai and his son, Gary Tsai, for using their Taiwan-based companies to export U.S.-origin goods and machinery that could be used by North Korea to produce weapons of mass destruction. Documents reported that in June 2008, Alex Tsai had been indicted in Taiwan for illegally forging invoices and shipping restricted materials to North Korea, and he was convicted later that year. Still, he could travel internationally. In January 2009, the Department of the Treasury designated Alex Tsai and his two companies for supporting a North Korean company involved in weapons proliferation. The Treasury Department urged all governments to cut off this channel for North Korean procurement. The Department of the Treasury then imposed sanctions against Taiwan's Trans Multi Mechanics Company and its general manager, Chang Wen-Fu, for procurement of dual-use machinery for North Korea and links to Alex Tsai. The sanctions were effective on May 10 pursuant to Executive Order 13382, "Blocking Property of Weapons of Mass Destruction Proliferators and Their Supporters."[21]

The United States enacted the Comprehensive Iran Sanctions, Accountability, and Divestment Act (CISADA) of 2010 (P.L. 111-195) on July 1, 2010, which followed the U.N. Security Council Resolution 1929 of June against Iran's nuclear program. Like others, Taiwan also is expected to comply with U.S. sanctions on Iran for nuclear proliferation in Section 1245 of the National Defense Authorization Act (NDAA) for FY2012 (P.L. 112-81). Taiwan has not announced its own sanctions against dealings with Iran's oil and gas industry, though petroleum refiner CPC Corporation Taiwan is a state-owned enterprise. In any case, Taiwan cut the volume of imports of oil from Iran by 49% from 2010 to 2011. In 2012, Taiwan further cut the volume by 39%, importing $805 million worth of oil from Iran, the eighth-largest source of Taiwan's oil imports.

On June 11, 2012, Secretary of State Clinton announced that Taiwan and six other countries significantly reduced oil purchases from Iran and would not be subject to the NDAA's sanctions for a renewable period of 180 days. On December 7, 2012, the Secretary of State again decided to exempt financial institutions in Taiwan (and other countries) from the NDAA's sanctions for 180 days, based on further reductions in oil imports from Iran. American Institute in Taiwan (AIT) Deputy Director Brent Christensen said in December that U.S. exemptions showed Taiwan's

---

[20] *Taipei Times*, October 26, 2012; *Asahi*, Tokyo, November 24, 2012; *Wall Street Journal*, November 28, 2012.

[21] Treasury Department, "Treasury Targets Taiwanese Proliferators," January 16, 2009; U.S. District Court, Northern Illinois, Criminal Complaints for Alex Tsai, October 23, 2012, and Gary Tsai, April 19, 2013; U.S. Attorney's Office, Northern District of Illinois, "Taiwanese Father and Son Arrested for Allegedly Violating U.S. Laws to Prevent Proliferation of Weapons of Mass Destruction," May 6, 2013; Treasury Department, "Treasury Sanctions Taiwan Proliferators Linked to North Korea," May 10, 2013; *Federal Register*, May 29, 2013.

commitment to global security, while U.S. policy encourages Taiwan (like other partners) to continue reducing economic ties to Iran. Meanwhile, in November 2012, Taiwan's Dragon Aromatics petrochemical company (operating in the PRC) bought its first cargo of Iranian condensate (natural gas in liquid form) from the PRC's Zhuhai Zhenrong oil company (under U.S. sanctions for transfers of gasoline to Iran).[22] On June 5, 2013, the Secretary of State again exempted Taiwan (and other countries) from sanctions under the NDAA for FY2012. Major Taiwan shipping companies, Evergreen and Yang Ming, reportedly stopped dealing with Iran.[23]

Taiwan could increase counter-piracy security for and/or restrict its ships to reduce the burden on international anti-piracy naval operations in the Gulf of Aden. A bilateral matter involved a U.S. Navy ship and the death of the captain (Wu Lai-yu) of one of Taiwan's fishing boats in a NATO anti-piracy operation off Somalia on May 10, 2011. On July 23, the U.S. government provided a report from the U.S. Fifth Fleet of the Naval Forces Central Command based in Bahrain on the frigate USS *Stephen W. Groves'* (*SWG*) interdiction of the Taiwan-flagged fishing boat that had been hijacked in March 2010 and then used as a pirate mother-ship along with pirate skiffs to attack other ships for more than a year off the Horn of Africa. The U.S. Navy operated under the NATO-led Combined Task Force 508 to conduct an operation on May 10 against the mother-ship to disrupt further attacks. After compelling the pirates to surrender and boarding the ship, the Navy's crew found Wu deceased in his cabin. An investigation found that ammunition fired from the U.S. naval ship during the operation "inadvertently" killed him and three pirates. The naval crew then buried the captain at sea, laid to rest in his ship, which was sunk to prevent it from becoming a hazard to other ships. The United States expressed "regret" that the ship and its captain were lost in the protection of shipping against piracy and sent condolences to Wu's family. The U.S. Navy maintained that it conducted the counter-piracy operation "in accordance with existing rules of engagement and in compliance with international law." However, Taiwan persisted in protests, including a call from the Foreign Minister for U.S. compensation to Wu's family, which demanded $3 million. Taiwan's government could have been trying to deflect political criticism and demands for compensation from Wu's family, since the government, including the navy, apparently took few if any steps to rescue the boat's captives while they were held for over a year. Somali pirates captured another fishing ship from Taiwan in December 2010. A PLA Navy frigate sailing off Somalia took credit for the release of the ship's crew in July 2012, though Taiwan's Foreign Ministry attributed their release to a ransom and international assistance. In August 2013, the LY amended a law to allow private armed guards on Taiwan's ships. The PLA Navy again claimed to escort a cargo ship from Taiwan in the Gulf of Aden on October 1.

Concerning maritime disputes in East Asia, there is an issue of whether Taiwan serves as a helpful, stabilizing U.S. security partner. Taiwan has asserted itself as the ROC with sovereign claims and has sought international attention and inclusion in bilateral or multilateral discussions. The disputes in the South China Sea involve overlapping claims by Brunei, Malaysia, PRC, Philippines (a U.S. ally), Taiwan, and Vietnam. In the East China Sea, PRC and Taiwan claims conflict with those of Japan (another U.S. ally). U.S. concerns involve possible conflict between the PRC and Japan over their competing claims to the Senkaku Islands (called Diaoyu Islands by the PRC), which could bring U.S. involvement under the U.S.-Japan defense treaty. Taiwan, asserting itself as the ROC, also claims the islands as Diaoyutai. On June 27, 2012, Assistant Secretary of State Kurt Campbell confirmed at a public forum that the State Department has discussed with Taiwan U.S. concerns about whether it would work with the PRC in the South

---

[22] *Reuters*, November 13, 2012; *Taipei Times*, December 6, 2012.

[23] *Reuters*, July 1, 2013.

China Sea and that Taiwan assured that it would be careful. Another issue concerns any cross-strait coordination also in the East China Sea. Taipei's officials have insisted on a position of no cooperation with the PRC. Nevertheless, even if not with explicit coordination, the parallel actions of Taiwan have added pressure against Japan, a U.S. ally. Moreover, there are concerns that the PRC and Taiwan have taken actions that militarized or escalated tensions. At another event on December 4, Campbell said U.S. officials underscored the expectation that Taiwan not take steps to provoke misunderstandings or tensions over the Senkaku Islands.

President Ma has sought support for his "East China Sea Peace Initiative," announced on August 5, 2012, that reiterated the ROC's claim over the islands as the Diaoyutai Islands and called for joint development of resources and a code of conduct to address tension peacefully. The next month, President Ma called for parallel bilateral talks (Taipei-Tokyo, Taipei-Beijing, and Beijing-Tokyo) that might advance to trilateral talks. In his National Day address on October 10, Ma said that his proposed principles also would apply in the South China Sea. There, Taiwan claims the Pratas Islands, Paracel Islands, Macclesfield Bank, and Spratly Islands, occupying since 1956 the largest one of the Spratly Islands (Taiping Island, or Itu Aba). Since 2000, Taiwan has stationed coast guard instead of military personnel on the island. Still, the military has supplied weapons to and trained the coast guard. In April 2013, Taiwan held a live-fire drill with some mortars and grenade launchers on the island. In August, Taiwan announced a budget of about $111 million to build a new pier in 2014-2016 and extend the runway on the island to support military ships and aircraft. The PRC's U-shape, nine-dash line (drawn as a "national border") in its maps of the South China Sea is a legacy of the ROC's maps from the 1940s. One question is whether Taipei would clarify the meaning of the controversial line consistent with international law.

Taiwan gave mixed messages. On September 25, the very day that the PRC and Japan held diplomatic exchanges to try to cool tensions as the United States urged, Taiwan deployed 12 Coast Guard ships to escort about 60 fishing boats into the Senkaku Islands' territorial waters. Reportedly, Japan's Coast Guard ships fired water cannons at Taiwan's fishing boats in the territorial waters, but Taiwan's Coast Guard ships fired water cannons toward Japan's official ships. The ships maneuvered in proximity, raising the risk of accidental collisions or endangerment of lives and property. However, while the media focused on the coast guard, Taiwan also deployed military assets. According to Taiwan's military news media, the military deployed two Knox-class frigates, one Perry-class frigate, F-16 fighters, Mirage fighters, E2-K Hawkeye airborne early warning aircraft, and S-70C ship-borne helicopters (a civilian version of the UH-60 Black Hawk). The United States sold to Taiwan such weapon systems (except for the Mirage fighters sold by France) for Taiwan's self-defense against the PRC. The next day, President Ma visited military units and praised the actions of the boats sailing close to the islands. Ma said that Japan "misappropriated" the islands for 117 years and never returned them.

Congress passed the FY2013 NDAA (enacted on January 2, 2013, as **P.L. 112-239**) with Section 1286 (based on an amendment by Senator Jim Webb) to express the sense of the Congress concerning the Senkaku Islands. Congress declared that the peaceful settlement of disputes in the East China Sea requires the exercise of self-restraint by all parties in activities that would complicate or escalate disputes and destabilize the region. The language, *inter alia*, stressed that while the United States takes no position on the ultimate sovereignty of the Senkaku Islands, the United States acknowledges the administration of Japan over the islands. Further, the legislation reaffirmed the U.S. commitment to Japan under Article V of the Treaty of Mutual Cooperation and Security that addressed an armed attack in the territories under Japan's administration. On January 18, Secretary of State Clinton added U.S. opposition to any unilateral actions that would seek to undermine Japan's administration and urged all parties to prevent incidents.

On January 24, 2013, Taiwan sent four Coast Guard ships to "escort" a boat close to the Senkaku Islands, though it sailed with protestors and a TV reporter (not fishermen). Japan's Coast Guard responded. Taiwan's military said that it strengthened air and naval patrols in the area. Taiwan's Coast Guard also warned the PRC's maritime surveillance ships to leave the area, likely concerned about political embarrassment if the PRC claimed to "protect" Taiwan's ships. Still, Taiwan already has faced the PRC's claim of "protecting" Taiwan's ships in the Gulf of Aden.

Nonetheless, Taiwan and Japan placed priority on concluding a long-awaited agreement over fishing rights near the Senkaku Islands. Negotiations started in 1996. Taiwan and Japan held their 16th round of talks in February 2009. On April 10, 2013, they held their 17th round of formal talks and signed a bilateral agreement that defined an expanded area for joint fishing rights. The agreement did not address the islands' 12-nm territorial sea and set up a commission to institutionalize discussions over disputes. The agreement was not unique but seemed to be a model of tension-reduction. President Ma credited his "East China Sea Peace Initiative" for the agreement and said that it did not prejudice either side's claims to sovereignty over the islands. The opposition DPP Chairman Su Tseng-Chang called the agreement an accomplishment. Japan reportedly was concerned about facing Taiwan-PRC unity amid heightened tensions. On April 23, AIT Chairman Ray Burghardt positively said that the agreement was handled well by both Taiwan and Japan. In several occasions starting on May 14, Japan's Coast Guard reportedly detained Taiwan's fishing boats for operating outside the agreed area, while Taipei's officials calmly urged fishermen to comply with the agreement rather than raising tension with Tokyo.

Aside from Japan, Taiwan faced increased tension with another democratic neighbor. On May 9, 2013, the Coast Guard of the Philippines (another U.S. treaty ally) shot at a Taiwan fishing boat (Guang Da Xing 28), resulting in the death of a Taiwan fisherman (Hong Shi-cheng), in the Luzon Strait between Taiwan and the Philippines. Taiwan's initial diplomatic reaction called for an investigation and arrests, and expressed grave concerns. However, the PRC quickly and harshly "condemned" the "barbaric act." This intervention likely placed pressure on Taiwan's leaders, who are said to fear political embarrassment if the PRC send ships to "protect" Taiwan's citizens or demand direct interactions with Manila under a "one China" policy. President Ma also faced stubbornly low approval ratings and a bid for re-election as the KMT Chairman on July 20.

The State Department reacted calmly the next day by welcoming the Philippines' pledge to hold a full and transparent investigation along with Taiwan and by urging all sides to ensure maritime safety and refrain from actions that could escalate tensions and undermine a diplomatic or peaceful resolution. (Similarly, in May 2010, Taiwan had urged restraint by both South Korea and North Korea in not escalating tension, when South Korea issued findings that its naval ship (Cheonan) was sunk and 46 sailors were killed by North Korea two months earlier.) President Ma initially said that Taiwan's Coast Guard (rather than the Navy) covered the interests of fishermen. Then on May 11, President Ma held a meeting of the National Security Council (NSC) and issued four demands of Manila: an official apology, compensation for losses, investigation and punishment, and negotiations over an agreement on fishing rights. Ma also issued an ultimatum that if the Philippines failed to meet the demands in 72 hours, by midnight on May 15, Taiwan would impose three sanctions: freezing the processing of applications of Filipino workers, recalling Taiwan's envoy, and requesting that Manila's envoy return to help resolve the dispute. On May 12 in Manila, Deputy Presidential Spokesperson, Abigail Valte, said that the Philippines' representative in Taipei, Antonio Basilio, visited the victim's family and "offered his apologies on behalf of the Philippine government." She also said that "as the Philippine Coast Guard has stated, we express our heartfelt sorrow on the unfortunate situation that occurred during one of the anti-illegal fishing patrols conducted by a Philippine fishery law enforcement vessel (MCS

3001) within the maritime jurisdiction (waters off the Batanes group of islands) of the Philippines on the morning of May 9, which tragically resulted in the death of a fisherman from one of the fishing vessels reportedly poaching in the area." However, Taiwan protested that Valte's statement did not contain a formal, government-to-government apology.

Meanwhile, by May 12, Taiwan increased Coast Guard patrols and sent the Navy's Lafayette-class and Knox-class frigates to "protect fishermen" between the island and the Philippines. The next day, Taiwan's Ministry of National Defense (MND) announced that it will send a Kidd-class destroyer and Perry-class frigate to join the Coast Guard in drills south of Taiwan on May 16. The Navy also said it would extend its patrol area by about 100 miles southward to the waters near the Batanes islands of the Philippines. The State Department, on May 13, expressed regret for the "tragic death" of the Taiwan fisherman and urged all parties to refrain from provocative actions. Reflecting the public's indignant nationalistic anger in the LY, Taiwan legislators across party lines supported Ma's demands. There was concern about violent targeting of Filipinos in Taiwan.

On May 15, President Ma held another NSC meeting, said that the Philippines failed to meet his demands by the deadline, and ordered the implementation of the three sanctions. A Deputy Minister of Justice said that an initial investigation by local prosecutors in Pingtung found 45 bullet holes in the boat's cabin where the crew sought cover and indicated the "deliberate killing" of the fisherman. Philippines President Benigno Aquino sent a "personal representative," Amadeo Perez, to Taiwan to apologize to the fisherman's family and Taiwan's people. On the night of May 15, Taiwan announced eight more sanctions (for a total of 11 measures): suspensions of normal travel (with an alert), high-level exchanges, economic exchanges, agricultural or fisheries cooperation, technical cooperation, talks on aviation, and visa-free treatment; and a military-coast guard drill. The State Department expressed concern about the increase in tensions between two neighboring democracies and U.S. partners. Taipei rejected Manila's apology as not formal, "nongovernmental," and insincere. On May 16, Taiwan proceeded with the Navy and Air Force exercise, sending a Kidd-class destroyer, a Lafayette-class frigate (with S-70C helicopters), two Mirage 2000 fighters, Indigenous Defense Fighters, and E-2K early warning aircraft. Naval ships sailed south of 20 degrees north latitude, the traditional line of patrol by the Coast Guard, and entered waters around the Batanes Islands. Taiwan's military said it did not use live ammunition.

Even as the investigations were ongoing, President Ma declared on May 17 that the shooting was "cold-blooded murder." PRC official media, including *CCTV* news programs, used the tension and Ma's rhetoric to condemn the Philippines and called for cross-strait actions in support of Taiwan's sanctions. Hackers from Taiwan and the Philippines reportedly exchanged cyber disruptions of government websites. Taiwan's officials called for calm treatment of Filipinos in Taiwan, while Taiwan's sanctions targeted Filipino workers and officials discouraged private, people-to-people ties, including volunteers going to help in the Philippines.

On May 19, Taiwan's Ministry of Justice reported that the fishing boat had 45 bullet holes. Based on their Agreement on Mutual Legal Assistance in Criminal Matters, Taiwan and the Philippines agreed to conduct "parallel investigations," after the Philippines rejected a "joint investigation" as violating its sovereignty. Respective investigators were in Taipei and Manila on May 27-31. Taiwan's investigators returned to Manila for talks on June 6-7. Reportedly, issues included the precise location and jurisdiction of the incident (reportedly about 40 miles east of the Philippines' northern Balintang Island), and specific charges against the Coast Guard officers.

On May 28, President Ma participated in an annual computerized military war game that focused on crisis-management in scenarios in the East and South China Seas (not the Taiwan Strait). Ma also announced on June 11 that the Navy and the Coast Guard will increase patrols in the South China Sea and that "protecting fishermen" will be another major mission of Taiwan's military.

Concerning talks on a fisheries agreement, Taiwan and the Philippines held their first preparatory meeting in Manila on June 14, and both sides, *inter alia*, agreed to avoid the use of force in patrols. In addition to their agreement on mutual legal assistance, there is another precedent for a bilateral agreement. In 2005, the Minister and Secretary of Agriculture of Taipei and Manila, through representatives, signed a Memorandum of Understanding to promote cooperation in agriculture and fisheries, including helping to prevent poaching on the waters of both sides. (The two sides later held their first formal talks in October 2013 and agreed to set up a hotline.)

On August 7, the Philippines reported on its investigation that recommended charges of homicide against eight Coast Guard officers and charges of obstruction of justice against four others. Taiwan issued its report, saying that local prosecutors in Pingtung also charged the eight officers with homicide. The Philippines' President sent an envoy to Taiwan to convey an apology and offer of compensation to the fisherman's family. The next day, Taiwan lifted its sanctions.[24]

Meanwhile, the Senate passed **S.Res. 167** (Menendez) on July 29, 2013. The resolution, *inter alia*, stated that the United States has a clear interest in encouraging and supporting nations to work collaboratively and diplomatically to resolve disputes in the Asia-Pacific maritime domains without coercion, without intimidation, without threats, and without the use of force. It noted that the fisheries agreement between Japan and Taiwan could be a model for other agreements. It urged all parties to exercise self-restraint to avoid undermining stability or escalating disputes.

International Space and Organizations

Taipei is a full member in some international organizations to which the PRC also belongs, such as the Asian Development Bank (ADB) and the WTO. Still, Taiwan has sought international space amid continued constraints from the PRC. Taiwan has been a full member of the Asian-Pacific Economic Cooperation (APEC) forum. For the second time since initiating APEC summits in Seattle in 1993, the United States hosted an APEC summit in 2011 in Honolulu. However, Taiwan's president has not been able to attend any of the APEC summits. The PRC has continued to block Taiwan's participation at international meetings or organizations. On November 14, 2013, Gambia ended its diplomatic recognition of the ROC, surprising the Ma Administration, which defended its "diplomatic truce" with the PRC (whereby Taipei and Beijing suspended vying for diplomatic relationships in a zero-sum game). The PRC insisted that it had no prior contact with Gambia and that it would work with Taiwan on their cross-strait ties.

---

[24] Author's observations, and numerous official and news reports including Taipei Economic and Cultural Office (TECO) and the Manila Economic and Cultural Office (MECO), Memorandum of Understanding on Agricultural and Fishery Cooperation, September 30, 2005; Taiwan Ministry of Foreign Affairs (MOFA), May 9; *Xinhua*, May 9; PRC Ministry of Foreign Affairs, May 10; *CNA*, May 10; *South China Morning Post*, May 11; President Ma's office, May 11; Taiwan MOFA, May 11; *GMA News*, May 12; Taiwan MOFA, May 12; *CNA*, May 12; *CNA*, May 13; *Taipei Times*, May 14; *Taipei Times*, May 15; President Ma's office, May 15; *CNA*, May 15; *GMA News*, May 15; *CNA*, May 15; *CNA*, May 16; Taiwan, "Non-Paper," May 16; Taiwan's MAC, May 16; *China Post*, May 17; *CNA*, May 17; *Philstar*, May 18; *Global Times*, article and editorial, May 18-19; *CNA*, May 19; *Philstar*, May 20; *Bloomberg*, May 21; Taiwan MOFA, May 22; *Philstar*, May 27; *CNA*, May 27; *CNA*, May 28; *Taipei Times*, May 29; *Taiwan News*, May 31; *Inquirer*, May 31; *CNA*, June 6; *GMA News*, June 6; *Taipei Times*, June 12; *CNA*, June 15, 2013; *Philstar*, August 7, *CNA*, August 7, Taiwan's MOFA, *Taiwan Today*, August 7, *Philstar*, August 8, and *CNA*, August 8, 2013.

The Clinton Administration's 1994 Taiwan Policy Review promised to support Taiwan's membership in organizations where statehood is not a prerequisite and to support opportunities for Taiwan's voice to be heard in organizations where its membership is not possible. The focus of congressional action for many years was on Taiwan's international participation at the World Health Organization (WHO) and the annual meetings in Geneva of its governing body, the World Health Assembly (WHA). On April 21 and May 6, 2004, the House and Senate passed H.R. 4019 and S. 2092 in support of Taiwan's efforts to gain observer status in the WHO and to make it an annual requirement to have an unclassified report from the Secretary of State on the U.S. plan to help obtain that status for Taiwan. One implication of this legislative change was the end of annual congressional statements and votes on this issue. In signing S. 2092 into law (P.L. 108-235) on June 14, 2004, President Bush stated that the United States fully supported the participation of Taiwan in the work of the WHO, including observer status.

President Ma decided to be more flexible than his DPP predecessor in pressing Taiwan's bid to rejoin the United Nations (U.N.), which it left in 1971 (as the ROC). On August 14, 2008, Taiwan submitted instead a letter (via some countries with which Taiwan has diplomatic relations) to allow Taiwan to "participate meaningfully" in U.N. specialized agencies.[25]

Only after Ma Ying-jeou was inaugurated as President in May 2008 did the WHO in January 2009 include Taiwan in the International Health Regulations (IHR). At the WHA in May 2009, Taiwan's Minister of Health participated, as an observer, for the first time since the ROC lost membership in the U.N. However, there have been concerns that the invitation had required the PRC's approval, came through a WHO-PRC memorandum of understanding (MOU), and was ad hoc (not routine for every year or only for a KMT President). Indeed, in its required report submitted to Congress in April 2010, the State Department reported that the WHO invited Taiwan to attend the 2009 WHA after the PRC "agreed to Taiwan's participation." Moreover, in May 2011, a secret WHO Memorandum (dated September 14, 2010) came to light in Taiwan, showing that the WHO had an "arrangement with China" to implement the IHR for the "Taiwan Province of China" (instead of "Chinese Taipei"). At the WHA on May 17, 2011, Secretary of Health and Human Services Kathleen Sebelius protested to the WHO, saying that no organization of the U.N. has a right to unilaterally determine the position of Taiwan.[26]

In its April 2013 report to Congress, the State Department stressed that the unresolved issue of nomenclature continued to hamper Taiwan's effective implementation of the IHR and that the WHO's communication with Taiwan was delayed by routing through PRC authorities in Beijing or Geneva. Taiwan must communicate with the WHO in an inconvenient and limiting way only through the WHO Legal Counsel. While Taiwan's experts were harassed or banned in accessing the WHA in 2011, U.S. diplomacy helped to prevent such incidents in 2012. Still, limits on Taiwan's participation in technical meetings remained unsatisfactory. The State Department stated a concern that Taiwan's sporadic and intermittent participation in the WHO limits Taiwan's ability to deal with health emergencies. In the same month, after Taiwan reported its first case of human infection of the PRC-origin H7N9 "bird flu," Taiwan protested to the WHO for incorrectly naming Taiwan as "Taiwan, China" on the WHO's reports on the H7N9 outbreak.

---

[25] United Nations General Assembly, A/63/194, "Need to Examine the Fundamental Rights of the 23 Million People of the Republic of China (Taiwan) to Participate Meaningfully in the Activities of the United Nations Specialized Agencies," dated August 22, 2008.

[26] The interpretation of Taiwan as a "province of China" is contrary to the U.N.'s own General Assembly Resolution 2758 of 1971, which "restored" the legal rights of the PRC in the U.N. and expelled "the representatives of Chiang Kai-shek" but did not mention Taiwan.

Deputy Assistant Secretary of State David Shear stated in March 2010 that "the United States is a strong, consistent supporter of Taiwan's meaningful participation in international organizations." He also stated that "Taiwan should be able to participate in organizations where it cannot be a member, such as the World Health Organization, the International Civil Aviation Organization, and other important international bodies whose activities have a direct impact on the people of Taiwan." Taiwan has sought status as an observer in the International Civil Aviation Organization (ICAO) and U.N. Framework Convention on Climate Change (UNFCCC). Taiwan's airlines (China Airlines, Eva Air, and TransAsia Airways) are members of the International Air Transport Association (IATA). Taiwan's Flight Safety Foundation provides indirect communication between domestic aviation authorities and airlines and the ICAO based in Montreal. In 2011, Taiwan joined the Civil Air Navigation Services Organization (CANSO), which is an observer in ICAO. Many believe that Taiwan's direct communication with ICAO would enhance international aviation security and safety. In July 2013, President Ma said that over 1.3 million flights pass through Taiwan's controlled airspace each year. Taiwan's challenges include justifying the practical gains, offering contributions, and gaining PRC support.

While the State Department initially stopped short of publicly supporting Taiwan's observer status in ICAO, Congress has supported this stance in passing legislation since 2010. On June 18 and 19, 2013, the House and Senate, respectively, passed H.R. 1151 (Royce) and S. 579 (Menendez), to direct the Secretary of State to develop a strategy to obtain observer status for Taiwan at ICAO. The House passed H.R. 1151 (by 424-0), after Representatives Royce, Faleomavaega, Ros-Lehtinen, and Green spoke in favor. The Senate passed H.R. 1151 (by unanimous consent) on June 27. President Obama signed the bill into law (**P.L. 113-17**) on July 12. He issued a statement of support for Taiwan's participation at ICAO, while construing the act to be consistent with the "one China" policy. On August 28, the State Department submitted a report as required by Section 1(c) of the legislation. The State Department told Congress of U.S. support for "observer status" for Taiwan in all of the meetings of ICAO. The report pointed to the ICAO Council, which meets regularly, in comparison with the ICAO Assembly, which meets triennially. The State Department noted that U.S. support for Taiwan in ICAO is consistent with the "one China" policy and the TRA. On September 13, AIT welcomed an announcement that the ICAO Council's President invited Taiwan's civil aviation officials to participate at the 2013 ICAO Assembly as "guests" of the ICAO Council's President. This invitation would allow Taiwan's participation at the 2013 ICAO Assembly. However, Taiwan did not become an "observer" at the ICAO Council or Assembly, and the invitation seemed *ad hoc* (for this meeting). On September 20, Chairman Royce of the Foreign Affairs Committee wrote a letter to the ICAO's Secretary General to express concerns that ICAO denied direct accreditation to Taiwan's reporters. (They later had to join Taiwan's official delegation to cover the event.) Reportedly based on an idea proposed by the PRC and announced by its Civil Aviation Administration, Taiwan attended the ICAO Assembly (held once in three years) as a "guest" from September 24 to October 4 in Montreal, Canada. The State Department issued a statement on September 24 to welcome ICAO's invitation to Taiwan and attributed the development to "international cooperation" and the support of ICAO and its members, rather than China's role.

Aside from various bilateral or multilateral negotiations that can be protracted and unpredictable, some analysts have argued that Taiwan could take unilateral steps to expand its international space and enhance its security. Taiwan could adjust its policies to be an attractive commercial center. U.S. businesses have stressed that Taiwan could be a prime location for investments.[27]

---

[27] Dan Blumenthal, Rupert Hammond-Chambers, Michael Mazza, Gary Schmitt, and Derek Scissors, "Taiwan, Inc.," (continued...)

Arms Sales to Taiwan

The Defense Department has reported to Congress in annual reports on the PLA that the balance of forces across the Taiwan Strait has continued to shift to the PRC's favor. Moreover, the Secretary's report of March 2009 told Congress that it was no longer the case that Taiwan's Air Force enjoyed dominance of the airspace over the strait. Since 2001, Taiwan has discussed the acquisition of diesel-electric submarines. Since 2006, Taiwan has been unsuccessful in trying to submit a formal request to procure new F-16C/D fighters. One policy issue concerns whether President Obama denied or delayed arms sales out of concern about military exchanges and other aspects of the overall relationship with the PRC. The Administration maintains that it adheres to the TRA. While the PRC has not warned Taiwan of consequences in continuing to seek U.S. weapons, the PRC has claimed to "suspend" many military meetings with the United States. President Obama notified Congress on January 29, 2010, of major arms sales to Taiwan: five programs with a total value of $6.4 billion. Again submitting notifications on one day, President Obama proposed on September 21, 2011, three major arms sales programs with a total value of $5.9 billion, including upgrades for Taiwan's existing F-16A/B fighters. Like Bush, President Obama has not notified Congress of the submarine design program (the only one pending from decisions in 2001) and has not accepted Taiwan's formal request for new F-16C/D fighters.

The United States has concerns that Taiwan under President Ma has not given sufficient priority to investing in defense. Taiwan cut its defense budget in 2009, 2010, and 2011 until an increase in 2012. The 2013 budget ($10.5 billion) is a small drop from that in 2012. Ma's Administration proposed a 2014 defense budget at the same level as the 2013 budget and would make up 2.0% of GDP. Ma has failed to reach the promised defense spending at 3% of GDP, even as Taiwan's military shifts from conscripts to volunteer personnel. There are increasing concerns about whether Taiwan's military is hollowing out, partly due to problems in recruitment and retention while shifting to a volunteer force by 2015 without sufficient investment and commitment by the leadership. On July 20, 2013, an estimated 30,000 demonstrators protested at the MND, after the death of a corporal on July 4 reportedly from heatstroke and abuse while in detention. The incident triggered another demonstration on August 3 by an estimated 100,000-250,000 protestors against the government's handling of this and other cases. Even before the protests that could harm recruitment and retention, MND reached only 14% of its recruitment goal for the first half of the year. The next month, the government delayed full conversion to a volunteer force for two years, or by 2017. On October 3, Deputy Assistant Secretary of State Kin Moy encouraged Taiwan to increase its defense budget to a level commensurate with its security challenges.

In the 113th Congress, on January 25, 2013, Representative Ileana Ros-Lehtinen introduced H.R. 419, the Taiwan Policy Act of 2013. The bill, *inter alia*, would seek to strengthen Taiwan's defense by authorizing a number of arms sales, acceptance of Taiwan's letter of request for F-16C/D fighters, and a sale of excess U.S. Navy Perry-class frigates as Excess Defense Articles (EDA). The bill also would require the Departments of Defense and State to brief and report to Congress on arms sales and the implementation of the TRA. On February 26, Senator Daniel Coats introduced S. 12, the Naval Vessel Transfer Act of 2013, to authorize the sale of excess Perry-class frigates to Taiwan. Representative Robert Andrews wrote a letter, dated June 4, to Defense Secretary Chuck Hagel, asking about possible U.S. support for Taiwan's indigenous submarine program. The Defense Department's response acknowledged that the United States has

---

(...continued)

AEI, October 2012; and American Chamber of Commerce (AmCham) in Taipei, "Taiwan White Paper," June 2013.

reviewed since 2008 Taiwan's request for a submarine design and noted that Taiwan has not requested technical assistance for a submarine program. The House, on June 14, passed H.R. 1960 (McKeon), NDAA for FY2014, with Section 1265 to direct the President to sell 66 F-16C/D fighters (approved as language offered by Representative Connolly for amendments en bloc). The Senate's report (S.Rept. 113-44) for the NDAA, S. 1197, extended the deadline to July 15, 2013, for the Defense Department to brief on Taiwan's air power and directed the department to submit a classified report on Taiwan's air force by December 1. (The briefing was required by April 15 in the conference report for the NDAA for FY2013, and it took place on July 17.)

Representative Michael McCaul sent a letter to Defense Secretary Hagel on September 5, 2013, asking about adherence to the TRA and Six Assurances, given a claim by the PLA's Director of the Foreign Affairs Office that visiting PRC Defense Minister Chang Wanquan and Secretary Hagel discussed a working group on arms sales to Taiwan. (Hagel and Chang did not say there would be such a working group in their press conference.) The next month, Under Secretary of Defense for Policy James Miller replied that the United States does not consult with China before deciding on arms sales to Taiwan and did not agree to do so when Hagel met with Chang. Miller noted adherence to the TRA but did not explicitly cite the Six Assurances. Also in October, Representative Randy Forbes led eight Members to send a letter to Secretary Hagel, urging him to invite Taiwan's military to participate in RIMPAC 2014 near Hawaii, after the United States invited the PLA Navy to participate at that multinational maritime exercise.[28] On November 12 and 13, Chairmen Menendez and Royce of the Senate Foreign Relations and House Foreign Affairs Committees introduced **S. 1683** and **H.R. 3470**, which would, *inter alia*, authorize the sale to Taiwan of up to four Perry-class frigates as Excess Defense Articles of the U.S. Navy. (Also see CRS Report RL30957, *Taiwan: Major U.S. Arms Sales Since 1990*, by Shirley A. Kan.)

Visa Waiver Program (VWP)

As one of its top priorities, Taiwan sought inclusion in the U.S. Visa Waiver Program (VWP), which eliminates some visa requirements for qualified countries, allowing their citizens to make temporary U.S. visits without first obtaining a valid visa. VWP countries must meet certain criteria, such as offering reciprocal privileges to U.S. citizens, having machine-readable passports, and having a low non-immigrant refusal rate.

The Ma Administration has stressed visa waiver status as a benefit for Taiwan's travelers, a symbol of support for his policies, and a step to support Taiwan's international stature. Mariko Silver, Acting Assistant Secretary of Homeland Security for International Policy, visited Taiwan in April 2010 and welcomed Taiwan's adoption of e-passports and looked to Taiwan's resolution of technical security and a new requirement for in-person applications for passports to prevent fraud. The refusal rate for Taiwan's applicants of U.S. non-immigrant visas was at 2.2% in 2010, better than the 3% standard for the VWP. In late 2010, Taiwan announced that it would sign three relevant agreements with the United States to exchange information on stolen or counterfeit passports, on terrorists, and on combating crime. Even without U.S. leadership in waiving visas for Taiwan's travelers, President Ma announced in June 2011 that Taiwan had secured offers from 116 countries and territories to grant its citizens visa-free or landing visa travel privileges. To prevent fraud, Taiwan started on July 1, 2011, a new system to require first-time applicants for

---

[28] Letter signed by Representatives Randy Forbes, Mike McIntyre, Rob Wittman, Madeleine Bordallo, Steve Chabot, Eni Faleomavaega, Michael McCaul, and Robert Brady, to Secretary of Defense Charles Hagel, October 21, 2013.

passports to apply in person. One implication of Taiwan's gaining visa waiver status was that approximately $15 million would be needed to offset visa processing fees lost per year to the State Department (starting in FY2013). With broader implications for more visitors, Assistant Secretary of Commerce Kumar said in Taiwan in September 2011 that almost 300,000 visitors from Taiwan contributed over $1 billion to the U.S. economy in 2010. On December 22, 2011, the State Department announced the nomination of Taiwan as a candidate for the VWP. The Department of Homeland Security then reviewed Taiwan's candidacy, including through a visit to Taiwan in March 2012 (vs. the higher-profile announcement of candidacy). Once Taiwan was included in the VWP, only Taiwan's e-passports would be eligible. Another issue for resolution concerned Taiwan's category of passports issued to "compatriots" whom Taiwan has not accepted for repatriation or given the right of residency (with questions about their true citizenship). On October 2, 2012, the Secretary of Homeland Security designated Taiwan in the VWP, effective on November 1. Taiwan's citizens may travel to the United States for business or tourism for up to 90 days without a visa. Taiwan became the 37th country to join the VWP. In December, more than 20,000 visitors from Taiwan came to the United States, an increase of 34% compared to the previous December. However, in the first nine months of 2013, Taiwan's visitors to the United States numbered 296,526 and showed a decline of 17% compared to the same period in 2012.

Other options could include Taiwan's inclusion in the Department of Homeland Security's Trusted Traveler and Trusted Trader programs. The Department's Deputy Assistant Secretary Mark Koumans visited Taipei in December 2012. In his speech on supply chain security, Koumans said that increased security can help facilitate (rather than impede) travel and trade.

Extradition Treaty

Taiwan has asked for an extradition treaty or agreement, and negotiations started in 2010, involving the Departments of Justice and State. Taiwan reportedly has sought about 70 fugitives suspected of being in the United States. In August 2013, President Ma Ying-jeou visited Saint Kitts and Nevis and witnessed the signing of an extradition treaty (the ROC's 11th such treaty). Taiwan had proposed an extradition treaty with the United States as early as 1979. In December 1992, the Senate Governmental Affairs Subcommittee on Investigations recommended negotiation of an extradition agreement with Taiwan as soon as possible. A precedent for congressional consideration could be the U.S.-Hong Kong extradition agreement.[29] Aside from an extradition treaty or agreement, another option could be authorizing statute passed by Congress. (Also see CRS Report 98-958, *Extradition To and From the United States: Overview of the Law and Recent Treaties*, by Michael John Garcia and Charles Doyle.)

Human Rights and Rule of Law

The TRA reaffirmed that the preservation and enhancement of the human rights of all of Taiwan's people are U.S. objectives. President Ma has contended that he has valued democracy, freedom, and human rights. However, in early November 2008, Taiwan's police allegedly used heavy-handed measures against protestors in providing security for an official from Beijing, ARATS

---

[29] Senate Governmental Affairs Subcommittee on Investigations, a report on "The New International Criminal and Asian Organized Crime," S. Prt. 102-129, December 1992; Senate Foreign Relations Committee, report on the "U.S.-Hong Kong Extradition Treaty," Exec. Rept. 105-2, August 19, 1997; Senate Foreign Relations Committee, report on the "Agreement with Hong Kong on the Transfer of Sentenced Persons," Exec. Rept. 105-24, October 14, 1998.

Chairman Chen Yunlin. Freedom House called for an independent investigation. Taiwan sent officials to Washington to defend the police, acknowledging a U.S. role. Concerned observers say that Taiwan under the KMT has not done enough to promote those values in the PRC or judicial reforms in Taiwan. Some have questioned whether the Ma Administration has downplayed democracy promotion by the Taiwan Foundation for Democracy (TFD) and has been less welcoming to those attacked by Beijing, such as political dissidents, Tibetan leader Dalai Lama, Uighur leader Rebiya Kadeer, and Falun Gong practitioners.

Trials of former President Chen Shui-bian (who has been sentenced to prison for 20 years in ongoing cases for corruption but also found not guilty of other charges) heightened scrutiny of pre-indictment and pre-trial detentions, prosecutorial leaks, other misconduct, transparency of judicial procedures, and prisoners' freedom of speech. On November 12, 2008, which happened to be the day that ex-President Chen was first detained on charges of corruption, AIT Director Stephen Young expressed the U.S. expectation that Taiwan's judicial process be "transparent, fair, and impartial." Jerome Cohen, a legal scholar at NYU's School of Law who was Ma's professor at Harvard, has written critiques of Taiwan's judicial system as well as commended Ma's signing of the instruments of ratification of the International Covenant on Civil and Political Rights and International Covenant on Economic, Social, and Cultural Rights. He wrote that the prosecution of former President Chen was not a political vendetta by the KMT but showed that no one is above the law in Taiwan. Still, Cohen criticized judicial officials for a skit on "Law Day" in 2009 that mocked the detained Chen and restraints on Chen's ability to defend himself. In a meeting with Professor Cohen in May 2010, President Ma said that judicial officials took actions to reduce human rights concerns about Taiwan's detention system.[30] In his second inaugural address in May 2012, Ma acknowledged the continued need for judicial reform.

A number of U.S. and foreign former officials, activists, and academics have written several open letters to President Ma to express concerns that Taiwan's judiciary lacked political independence or objectivity. A letter of April 11, 2011, in the *Taipei Times* asked whether legal charges against 17 former DPP officials of the Chen Administration for allegedly failing to return about 36,000 documents were "politically motivated" in coming out three years after the transition in 2008 and during electoral campaigns. On June 30, 2011, prosecutors indicted Lee Teng-hui, who was president from 1988 to 2000, for allegedly diverting $7.8 million in diplomatic funds for the establishment of the Taiwan Research Institute in the 1990s. Some foreign observers questioned whether the legal action was timed to affect Lee's support for the DPP in the elections in January 2012 and noted the lack of prompt follow-up.[31] The first hearing on Lee's case was on June 22, 2012, but he could not attend until another hearing on August 10. On November 15, 2013, the Taipei District Court acquitted former president Lee of embezzlement. In contrast, a high-profile case against a ruling KMT politician, Lin Yi-shih, raised controversy, when the Taipei District Court, on April 30, 2013, found him not guilty of corruption and sentenced him to seven years in prison. Lin was charged with using his positions as a legislator and then Secretary-General of the Executive Yuan (Cabinet) to demand payments for contracts with a state-owned corporation. The Control Yuan (the government branch responsible for accountability) impeached Lin in June.[32]

---

[30] Jerome Cohen's articles published in *South China Morning Post*, Hong Kong, May 28, 2009, June 11, 2009, September 17, 2009, October 15, 2009, January 20, 2010; and *Apple Daily*, October 9, 2009.

[31] For example, see another open letter to President Ma Ying-jeou in the *Taipei Times* on August 2, 2011.

[32] *Taiwan News*, May 1, 2013; *Taipei Times*, May 1, 2013; *Central News Agency*, June 11, 2013.

In March-April 2012, some Members in Congress (including Representatives Steve Chabot, Dan Lungren, and Ed Royce) raised concerns about Chen's prison conditions and health. In July, Representatives Robert Andrews and Lungren submitted a report by medical professors at the University of California at Davis to the Tom Lantos Human Rights Commission, raising questions about the conditions of ex-President Chen in prison (confined in a small cell) and calling for his medical parole.[33] Chen's conditions in prison reportedly improved in June.

However, starting in September 2012, Chen's medical condition deteriorated, requiring extended guarded stays in hospitals. Taiwan's Ministry of Justice denied that political bias influenced Chen's medical care. In October, Representative Howard Berman wrote to President Ma, calling for Chen's release from prison on humanitarian grounds. Also, Senator Sherrod Brown wrote to the AIT Director in Taipei, asking him to visit Chen. Jerome Cohen met with Chen at a hospital in Taipei in December, showing concern about this medical treatment while declining to call for Chen's medical parole. In January 2013, Representative Steve Chabot added his support for Chen's medical parole. Representative Andrews wrote a letter on March 1 to Secretary of State John Kerry, strongly urging his department to take a stance on the treatment of Chen. Two weeks later, the State Department responded that AIT has raised concerns about Chen's health with Taiwan's officials. On April 19, the Justice Ministry suddenly moved Chen from the Veterans General Hospital in Taipei to Taichung Prison's Pei-Te Hospital (in the central city of Taichung), with a special area for Chen with a garden. The Justice Ministry argued that it has treated Chen legally and appropriately as a prisoner, medical patient, and former head of state. Some doctors, relatives, DPP politicians, and activists protested. The DPP called for Chen's medical parole. On May 2 in Taiwan, accompanied by AIT officials, Representatives Chabot and Eni Faleomavaega (of the House Foreign Affairs Subcommittee on Asia and the Pacific) visited Chen at Taichung Prison's hospital. Mr. Chabot said he offered his personal view about Chen's human rights.[34]

In April 2013, the State Department issued its worldwide human rights reports for 2012, noting that Taiwan's principal human rights problems concerned corruption and violence against women and children. The State Department also reported that the right to strike was highly regulated, and that there was evidence of forced labor and violations of maximum working hours.

Concerning human rights in China, in mid-November 2012, Taiwan's Foreign Ministry denied a visa to the Tibetan Dalai Lama to attend a conference in Taipei. Opposition DPP lawmakers criticized the decision that simply cited bad timing. Taiwan did not issue a policy statement. In contrast, the State Department confirmed on November 30 that Assistant Secretary for Human Rights Affairs Michael Posner met with relatives of Tibetans who self-immolated in the Tibetan area. The department then issued a statement on December 5 by Maria Otero, the U.S. Special Coordinator for Tibetan Issues. The United States expressed concern about violence and increasing self-immolations in the Tibetan areas, called on the PRC government to address policies, including use of force, that exacerbated the tensions, expressed hope that the self-immolations will end, urged the PRC to allow reporters, diplomats, and other observers to the Tibetan areas, and called on the PRC to talk with the Dalai Lama without preconditions. Taiwan last allowed the Tibetan leader and Nobel Peace Prize winner to visit in 2009, in the wake of a major typhoon. Congress and President Bush had awarded in the U.S. Capitol the Congressional Gold Medal to the Dalai Lama in October 2007.

---

[33] U.S. Citizen Medical Team (Joseph Lin, Ken Yoneda, and Charles Whitcomb), "The Effects of Incarceration on the Mental and Physical Health of Former President Chen Shui-bian of Taiwan," July 12, 2012.

[34] "U.S. Politicians Concerned About A-Bian," *Taipei Times*, May 4, 2013.

Taiwan allowed a visit by PRC activist Chen Guangcheng, who arrived in Taipei on June 24, 2013. The well-known blind human rights activist fled detention in China to the American Embassy, which negotiated his release in May 2012 for a one-year fellowship at NYU. Chen said that Taiwan presented a model in fighting for democracy. However, President Ma declined to meet with Chen, though Jerome Cohen accompanied him and his visit lasted 18 days.

Democratic Elections (KMT and DPP)

The United States has closely watched Taiwan's elections, because of the critical implications for U.S. interests in democracy and security. Taiwan held elections on January 14, 2012, with the first combined presidential and legislative elections on one day. Beijing seemed to favor incumbent President Ma Ying-jeou. The CPC and KMT oppose Taiwan's independence and agree on what they call now the "1992 Consensus." KMT President Ma won re-election with 51.6% of the votes, a victory of 6 percentage points over DPP Chairwoman Tsai Ing-wen, who won 45.6% of the votes. Voter turnout was lower than in previous elections but still considered high (74% out of 18 million eligible voters). Out of 113 seats in the Legislative Yuan (LY), the KMT won the majority with 64 (down from 72 seats), and the DPP won 40 seats (up from 32). Minor parties and an independent won the remaining 9 LY seats. The State Department congratulated Taiwan for another free and fair election. On August 2, 2012, Senator Lisa Murkowski introduced S.Res. 542 to express the sense of the Senate that the United States should continue to support democracy and human rights in Taiwan after the elections. The bill noted a report by a group of international observers that found the elections were "mostly free but only partly fair."[35]

Observers attributed DPP Chairwoman Tsai's loss to lack of clarity and certainty about how she would sustain the status quo and a stable cross-strait relationship. She tried to balance appeals to the pro-independence base and to moderate voters who support continued cross-strait economic engagement. While Tsai proposed a "Taiwan Consensus," the KMT touted "peaceful development" under the KMT-CPC's "1992 Consensus." Instead of a clearer stance on the ECFA signed in June 2010 amid a dwindling number of DPP-led protestors, Tsai said vaguely that she would use "democratic procedures" to continue the policy.[36] In October 2011, Tsai said "Taiwan is the ROC, the ROC is Taiwan." Tsai focused on income inequality, but Taiwan's economic conditions have been tied to the PRC's economy. Rather than keeping distance from Taiwan's electoral politics, in August 2011, Beijing opposed the DPP's policy guidelines as "unacceptable." On December 16, 2011, CPC Politburo Standing Committee Member Jia Qinglin warned that cross-strait talks would not continue without accepting the "1992 Consensus." Taiwan's major businesses with interests in mainland China echoed support for the "1992 Consensus." The DPP also attributed its loss to the Obama Administration's actions seen as favoring Ma. As a close U.S. observer told the *Washington Post* after the election, "the administration liked the fact that tensions had been reduced across the Taiwan Strait … and rewarded Ma."[37] While it was difficult to determine the impact of various factors, a poll taken after the elections indicated that the most cited concerns of voters were the economy, income gap, cross-strait ties, and social welfare.[38]

---

[35] On September 19, 2012, Senator Murkowski submitted to the *Congressional Record* the summary of the report of the International Election Observers Mission, written by Woodrow Clark and Frank Murkowski.

[36] Tsai Ing-wen's interview with *Apple Daily*, Taipei, September 20, 2010.

[37] Andrew Higgins, "Taiwan's Pro-China Chief Reelected," *Washington Post*, January 15, 2012, quoting Douglas Paal.

[38] *Chung-kuo Shih-pao (China Times)*, Taipei, January 16, 2012.

The DPP continues as a viable party in Taiwan's electoral politics, with observers watching for potential party unity and rejuvenation in leadership. After Chen Shui-bian's eight years in office, the DPP had suffered a significant loss in the presidential election in 2008. Nonetheless, the DPP under Chairwoman Tsai Ing-wen rebuilt its strength and won a number of local and legislative elections in 2009-2011. The DPP then lost to the KMT in the presidential election in 2012 but with a smaller margin than that in 2008, and the DPP gained seats in the LY. Tsai stepped down as the chair. Some observers have concerns about the DPP in future elections and any reversal of the warming trend in cross-strait ties. Others have confidence about the DPP's evolution as a party that provides democratic checks and balance and about the voters' choices on their status. While the KMT stresses the ROC's legacy that includes "one China," the DPP pursues Taiwan-centric policies based on a legacy of fighting for freedoms and a stated priority of ties to democratic countries like the United States and Japan. In contrast to the KMT's touting of the "1992 Consensus," the DPP says that cross-strait talks cannot be simply KMT-CPC negotiations.

Nonetheless, both the KMT and DPP could continue to use political ambiguity, including the KMT's use of "1992 Consensus." The KMT and DPP could find areas of common ground concerning the ROC's name and constitution, forging a domestic consensus about Taiwan's relationships with the United States, Japan, and the PRC, and protecting the way of life in the democratic, security, and economic interests of Taiwan's people. No matter which party rules, Taiwan faces challenges from the PRC within the context of economic integration. The DPP could clarify or review its approach toward the United States and toward the PRC.

After winning the election to be the DPP's chairman on May 27, 2012, former premier Su Tseng-chang (at age 64) announced restoration of the DPP's Department of "China Affairs," among various departments. While such a move took cross-strait policy out of "international" policy, the approach differed from the KMT and CPC's use of "mainland China." Not until later (in August) did Su set up a Department on Defense Policy. On October 4-8, former premier Frank Hsieh became the most senior member of the DPP to visit the PRC, though on a private visit. He met with senior PRC officials (State Councilor Dai Bingguo, ARATS Chairman Chen Yunlin, and TAO Director Wang Yi). Hsieh proposed a "constitutional consensus" ("two constitutions with different interpretations") for the "status quo," instead of talking about the "1992 Consensus" ("one China with different interpretations"). Hsieh's idea did not represent the DPP's proposal but represented an effort to review the party's policy on China. Hsieh urged the DPP to accept the ROC constitution. In November, DPP Chairman Su named himself as the convener of the higher-level Committee on China Affairs (later set up in May 2013 with members that include Hsieh).

The DPP has reached out to the United States, Japan, Singapore, the PRC, Canada, and other countries. At a cross-strait conference in Taipei in December 2012, a DPP official, Joseph Wu, met with TAO Deputy Director Sun Yafu, who reportedly said that talks should continue without preconditions. Chairman Su visited Japan in January 2013, stressing that Taiwan should not provoke tensions over the Senkaku (Diaoyutai) islands. On the eve of his visit to the United States in June, Chairman Su issued a DPP paper on defense policy. It stressed strengthening defense against the PRC, raising the defense budget to 3% of GDP, and cooperating with all democracies, but it expressed a consensus with the KMT on a "military presence" in the dispute with the Philippines over the shooting of a Taiwan fisherman in May. During his visit, Su met with Members of Congress, Administration officials, and others. Su's message was that Taiwan is a sovereign country that does not belong to the PRC, but he also said that seeking independence was unnecessary and that the country's name under the constitution is "Republic of China." He said that this is Taiwan's "status quo" and what he called the "Taiwan Consensus." Su said that Taiwan's relationship with the United States is the most important and needs to be strengthened.[39]

Restoring Trust and Resolving Disputes (Beef and Pork)

Taiwan has a window for greater attention to governance, before the local elections in 2014 and presidential election in 2016. Taiwan's political seasons have constrained U.S. influence on some priorities, particularly to relax Taiwan's restrictions on U.S. beef. Taiwan banned U.S. beef in 2003 and 2005 out of concern about bovine spongiform encephalopathy (BSE), or mad cow disease. In 2006, Taiwan lifted the ban but imposed restrictions on U.S. beef. U.S. concerns include whether Taiwan abides by rules of the WTO and World Organization for Animal Health (OIE), of which Taiwan is a member, even as Taiwan seeks U.S. support for its participation in international organizations. Taiwan has been a key market for U.S. beef exports, with values that increased from $42 million in 2005 to $215 million in 2010. The value dropped to $199 million in 2011 and dropped further to $128 million in 2012, according to the U.S. Meat Export Federation.

In April 2009, President Ma gave a speech directed at the Obama Administration, including a promise to open Taiwan's market to U.S. agricultural exports, alluding to the U.S. request conveyed to him since his inauguration day in May 2008 that Taiwan lift restrictions on U.S. beef. In October 2009, President Ma agreed to conclude two years of negotiations on an agreement to relax Taiwan's restrictions on imports of U.S. beef over Taiwan's concern about mad cow disease. The United States maintains that U.S. beef is safe. Under the U.S.-Taiwan agreement signed on October 22, 2009, Taiwan would allow bone-in beef, ground beef, and cow parts under 30 months of age without specified risk materials (skulls, spines, brains, etc.). However, both the ruling KMT and opposition DPP complained. In what the Ma Administration admitted as a "crisis," Taiwan raised tension with the Obama Administration and Congress over beef. Taiwan's Legislative Yuan passed in January 2010 a bill to ban ground beef, parts, and risky materials from areas with mad cow disease in the past 10 years. The USTR and Members of Congress expressed concerns about Taiwan's political, unscientific restrictions and questions of safety concerning U.S. beef, unilateral abrogation of an agreement, and violations of key principles in international trade that harmed U.S. agricultural exports. However, the broader U.S. business community questioned the freezing of TIFA talks due to one category of exports, and some observers pointed out that the United States has continued trade talks with the PRC in spite of many disputes.

Taiwan then raised another dispute over beef, right before an attempted resumption of TIFA talks expected in late January 2011. On January 15, Taiwan ordered the removal from sale of U.S. beef with a drug to promote leanness called ractopamine, although the United States maintains that the additive is safe. On February 17, the chairmen and ranking Members of the Senate Finance Committee and House Ways and Means Committee (Senators Max Baucus and Orrin Hatch, and Representatives Dave Camp and Sander Levin) wrote a letter to President Ma to express concern that U.S. beef exports to Taiwan stopped effectively, to urge a correction, and to seek confidence to resume the TIFA talks. On July 13, 2011, AIT expressed disappointment in Taiwan's apparently "political" decision to keep the ban by citing the lack of agreement at an international commission on acceptable, maximum residue levels (MRLs) for ractopamine. Representative Royce delivered a speech on November 12, in which he lamented that only with Taiwan (not

---

[39] DPP, press release on Su's remarks in New York, June 10; Su's speech at Brookings Institution, June 13, 2013.

South Korea and Japan) has the Administration suspended overall economic talks over the "narrow, politically-charged" dispute about beef.

With an expectation that President Ma would resolve the dispute after the January 2012 elections, AmCham in Taipei urged Ma to put an end to the dispute before it "further damages" the relationship with the United States. In February and March, AIT issued Fact Sheets about the safety of U.S. beef and ractopamine, which also pointed out that Taiwan itself has established MRLs for over 100 veterinary compounds. The Department of Commerce postponed the visit of Under Secretary Francisco Sanchez scheduled for March 4-6, amid protests, recalls of U.S. beef, and DPP and KMT proposals in the LY to stipulate zero-tolerance for ractopamine. President Ma held "national security" meetings over this "crisis." The Ma Administration then issued four conditions for beef: safe levels of ractopamine, separate allowances for beef and pork (amid objections from hog farmers), labeling of meats, and no imports of organs. To counter the domestic political pressure, Ma argued that a resolution was needed for U.S.-Taiwan ties and Taiwan's international integration to avoid marginalization.

On March 6, 2012, Senator Chuck Grassley issued a press release stating that he was encouraged by Taiwan's announcement that it would allow some beef imports containing ractopamine. But he added that there was no scientific reason for Taiwan to set residual levels of a certain additive for beef but not pork.[40] On March 15, 68 Members of Congress led by Representatives Denny Rehberg and Ron Kind sent a letter to the Secretary of Agriculture and the USTR, objecting to Taiwan's protectionist trade restrictions on U.S. pork and beef. They wrote that "further toleration of Taiwan's unnecessary restrictions sets a dangerous precedent for the mistreatment of U.S. products and undermines our efforts to establish objective, internationally-recognized science-based standards for U.S. exports."[41] Then, on April 24, the Department of Agriculture found a cow with mad cow disease, stating that it posed no risk. In the LY, some lawmakers of the ruling KMT voted down attempts by lawmakers of opposition parties led by the DPP to ban U.S. beef (including on April 27 and May 4, 11, and 18). A committee in the LY defeated on May 7 the Cabinet's proposal to allow beef with safe levels of ractopamine, leaving a potential vote in the full LY. Meanwhile, Taiwan sent agricultural officials who arrived on May 6 in Washington and then set up meetings with U.S. officials, associations, and beef processing sites. The officials visited several states over 23 days and found U.S. beef to be safe.

AmCham in Taipei complained that the dispute over beef had become "heavily politicized" but commended President Ma for doing the right thing in working on a resolution. Although the Speaker of the LY, Wang Jin-pyng of the KMT, negotiated an agreement between the KMT and DPP to extend the LY's session for two weeks until June 15, 2012, in part to vote on the Cabinet's, or Executive Yuan's (EY's), amendment to the Act Governing Food Safety, the LY did not vote by then. As KMT Chairman, Ma met with the LY's KMT Caucus on June 7 to forge party unity behind his proposal. Starting on June 11, DPP, TSU, and PFP opposition lawmakers occupied the Speaker's podium in the LY's chamber to prevent a vote all week, targeting what some called the "U.S. beef bill" as detrimental to food safety. The DPP's new chairman, Su Tseng-chang, visited the DPP legislators and supported their stance. Some DPP politicians claimed that they were not opposing U.S. beef yet denounced "toxic" or "poisonous" beef.

---

[40] Senator Chuck Grassley, "Taiwan Decision on U.S. Beef Imports Should Apply to Pork," March 6, 2012.

[41] Representative Denny Rehberg, "Rehberg Leads Ongoing Fight Against Unfair Trade Restrictions by Taiwan on U.S. Pork and Beef," March 15, 2012.

On July 5, Representatives Edward Royce and Gerald Connolly led 10 Members of Congress to write to President Obama to urge a resumption of the TIFA talks, while "Taiwan must take steps to open its market to U.S. agriculture exports."[42] On the same day, the international Codex Alimentarius Commission voted in Rome to adopt MRLs for ractopamine in beef and pork. The DPP cited that development to announce support for international standards and sought to rebuild trust with the United States. However, at a special session of the LY on July 25, all legislators in the DPP Caucus voted against the bill to end the ban on ractopamine in beef. In passing the KMT-supported bill (63-46), 40 DPP, 3 PFP, and 3 TSU legislators voted against it. While the DPP stopped obstructing the legislative process, its vote continued to raise questions about its political leadership and principles (professed to be in concert with Washington), when the elections were over in January and Taiwan's people commonly expressed satisfaction with U.S. products. The DPP defended its stance as part of supporting its own version of the legislation, which included language on differentiating between treatment of beef and pork, while resolving the dispute.

After the postponement of his visit in March, Under Secretary of Commerce Sanchez visited Taipei in late October 2012. He highlighted the start on November 1 of the VWP for Taiwan's travelers to facilitate their visits to the United States for tourism and business. Sanchez welcomed the news that U.S. beef was again available, a step to strengthen confidence in Taiwan as a responsible trading partner. However, Taiwan has maintained a ban on ractopamine for pork. At a hearing of the Senate Finance Committee on March 19, 2013, Senator Grassley expressed concern that Taiwan has continued to "discriminate against pork" with an "unjustifiable barrier" despite an expectation of a resolution after Taiwan's political elections (in January 2012).

Economic Issues[43]

Taiwan is a major innovator and producer of information and communication technologies (ICT), broadly defined as technologies that provide access to information through telecommunications, including the Internet, wireless networks, cell phones, and other communication mediums.[44] According to the Taiwan government, Taiwan firms located at home and abroad are the world's second-largest producer of ICT products.[45] About 83% of Taiwan ICT products are produced outside Taiwan—mainly China. In 2010, Taiwan's ICT industry generated $424.6 billion in revenues.[46] Numerous surveys have identified Taiwan as a major leader in global technology. For example:

- A *BusinessWeek* survey of the 100 best performing global information technology companies in 2009 listed 10 Taiwanese firms, 4 of which were among the world's top 10 technology firms.[47]

---

[42] Letter to Barack Obama from Representatives Edward Royce, Gerald Connolly, Donald Manzullo, Howard Berman, Gary Ackerman, Steve Chabot, Walter Jones, James Moran, Renee Ellmers, and Mike Kelly, July 5, 2012.

[43] Written by Wayne Morrison, Specialist in Asian Trade and Finance.

[44] *Techterms.com*.

[45] According to the U.S. Census Bureau, ICT equipment include central office switching equipment, telephones and telephone apparatus, facsimile equipment, bridges, routers, gateways, portable transmitting and receiving antennas, communication satellites, cable television equipment, global positioning system (GPS) equipment, radio and television studio broadcasting equipment, fire detection and alarm systems, and intercom systems.

[46] Taiwan Ministry of Economics and Digitimes, *Taiwan's ICT Industry Development and Outlook*, June 2011.

[47] Bloomberg Businessweek, *the InfoTech 100*, 2009, available at http://www.businessweek.com/interactive_reports/ (continued...)

- According to the World Bank's *Knowledge Economy Index* (KEI), which attempts to measure and rank a country's ability to generate, adopt, and diffuse knowledge, Taiwan ranked 13th out of 145 economies in 2012.[48]

- The World Economic Forum's *Global Information Technology Report* for 2012 ranked Taiwan 11th out of 142 economies in terms of preparedness to leverage ICT advances for increased competitiveness and development.[49]

Taiwan's Global Trade

Taiwan's economy is highly dependent on trade. In 2012, Taiwan's exports of goods and services were equal to 74% of gross domestic product (GDP). From 2005 to 2012, net exports (exports minus imports) were the largest contributor to Taiwan's annual GDP growth.[50] Taiwan's 2012 merchandise exports and imports were $284 billion and $271 billion, respectively, making it the world's 17th-largest exporter and 18th-largest importer. Continued weakness in the global economy has significantly impacted Taiwan's economy. Taiwan's real GDP grew 10.8% in 2010 over the previous year (while real exports of goods and services were up 25.6%).

In 2011, real GDP slowed to 4.1% (real exports of goods and services grew by 4.4%), and in 2012, real GDP increased by only 1.3% (real exports of goods and services experienced nearly zero growth). Taiwan's nominal GDP in 2012 was $475 billion.[51] Taiwan's top trading partners in 2012 were China, Japan, the United States, Singapore, and South Korea (see **Table 1**).

Table 1. Taiwan's Top Five Trading Partners: 2012

($ billions)

	Total	Exports	Imports	Trade Balance
World	**555.1**	**284.3**	**270.8**	**13.5**
China	121.6	80.7	40.9	39.8
Japan	64.7	17.1	47.7	-30.6
United States	55.4	31.8	23.5	8.3
Singapore	27.2	19.0	8.1	10.9
South Korea	26.6	11.5	15.1	-3.6

Sources: Data for China are from Taiwan's Mainland Affairs Council. All other data are from the Global Trade Atlas.

Note: Data on China are direct trade as well as estimated indirect trade through Hong Kong.

(...continued)

it100_2009 html.

[48] The World Bank, *the Knowledge Economy Index*, 2012, at http://info.worldbank.org/etools/kam2/KAM_page5.asp.

[49] See http://www.weforum.org/reports/global-information-technology-report-2012.

[50] For example, in 2011, Taiwan's real GDP grew by 4.0% over the previous year. The components of that growth were net exports (at 3.7 percentage points), private consumption (1.6%), and government consumption (0.2%), while stockbuilding and gross fixed investment declined by 0.8% and 0.7%, respectively.

[51] IHS Global Insight, *Country & Industry Forecasting, Taiwan*, March 1, 2013.

Taiwan has tried to expand trade, amid concerns about the proliferation of regional and bilateral FTAs that exclude Taiwan, especially among Taiwan's major trading partners and competitors. Taiwan's officials have warned that the exclusion of Taiwan from such FTAs could weaken the competitiveness of Taiwanese firms, diminishing trade and economic growth.[52] Currently, Taiwan has FTAs with only Panama, Nicaragua, El Salvador, Guatemala, and Honduras, which, together account for only a minor share of Taiwan's total trade. In contrast, South Korea, a major competitor for many Taiwanese exporters, has FTAs in effect with the United States, the European Union, the 10 countries of the Association of Southeast Asian Nations (ASEAN), Peru, India, the European Free Trade Association (EFTA), Singapore, and Chile. South Korea has concluded FTAs with Turkey and Columbia and is negotiating with 11 other countries and regions.[53] Until recently, Taiwan's efforts to enter into negotiations for an FTA with its major trading partners have proven unsuccessful, partly because of opposition by China.[54]

In an effort to boost economic ties with China in order to take advantage of its rapidly growing economy, and to improve the chances of Taiwan entering into FTAs with other countries,[55] the Ma Administration, after coming into office in 2008, sought to liberalize cross-strait trade and investment barriers. This included the lifting of restrictions on direct trade, transportation, and postal links.[56] In 2010, the two sides negotiated the Economic Cooperation Framework Agreement (ECFA), an FTA that seeks to significantly liberalize trade and investment barriers over time. The agreement is expected to hasten the pace of cross-strait economic integration and boost economic growth on both sides.[57] The agreement included an "early harvest" provision to eliminate tariffs on various products within three years.[58] As part of the ECFA process, the two sides reached an agreement in June 2013 to liberalize trade in services.

Press reports indicate that, since the signing of the ECFA, China has backed away somewhat from its opposition to Taiwan seeking trade agreements with other countries, which the Taiwan government calls "economic cooperation agreements" (ECAs).[59] On July 10, 2013, Taiwan reached an economic cooperation agreement (ECA) with New Zealand, and signed the

---

[52] For example, countries with FTAs often reduce most or all of their tariff levels to zero. Since Taiwan is not partner to of the FTA its products will be assessed the non-FTA tariffs, which could put them at a competitive disadvantage.

[53] Republic of Korea, Ministry of Foreign Affairs and Trade, FTA Status of ROK, at http://www.mofat.go kr/ENG/ policy/fta/status/overview/index.jsp?menu=m_20_80_10.

[54] In the past, PRC officials have argued that only "sovereign nations" can enter into FTAs, which, they claim, Taiwan is not because it is "part of China." However, WTO rules allow its members to negotiate FTAs. Taiwan is a member of the WTO under the title: "the Separate Customs Territory of Taiwan, Penghu, Kinmen, and Matsu (Chinese Taipei)."

[55] Another concern to Taiwan policymakers was China's FTA agreements with ASEAN, which is considered the world's largest FTA in terms of population, and third largest in terms of trade flows and GDP. The China-ASEAN Free Trade Area went into effect on January 1, 2010. Taiwan officials sought an ECFA with China to ensure that Taiwan's exports to China remained competitive vis-a-vis ASEAN exports to China.

[56] Until recently, most trade, transportation, and postal links with China occurred indirectly, mainly via Hong Kong. These constituted significant added time and money costs to cross-strait economic ties.

[57] During the debate over the ECFA, the Taiwan government argued that the agreement would greatly benefit Taiwan's economy, estimating that it would boost GDP by 1.7% and exports by 5.0%, and expand employment by 263,000. Taiwan opponents of the EFCA contended that the agreement would lead to further hollowing out of Taiwan's manufacturing industries, while other warned the agreement would make Taiwan overly-dependent on China's economy, which would give China leverage over Taiwan.

[58] China agreed to eliminate 539 items and Taiwan agreed to eliminate tariffs on 267 items.

[59] Taiwan's Ministry of Economic Affairs defines an ECA as "an agreement signed by two or more economies for promotion of trade activities and economic integration with each other by reducing tariffs and fees, as well as by eliminating other trade barriers for goods and services."

Agreement between Singapore and Taiwan on Economic Partnership (ASTEP) on November 7. Taiwan also has pursued exploratory talks with the European Union, the Philippines, India, Indonesia, and Israel about the possibility of an ECA.[60]

Taiwan has expressed interest in a FTA/ECA with the United States for the past several years. Some analysts have urged Taiwan to pursue other agreements with the United States, such as a bilateral investment agreement, which could boost both trade and investment.[61] In addition, Taiwan is seeking to join various proposed regional FTAs, including the Trans-Pacific Partnership (TPP) that would include the United States; and the Regional Comprehensive Economic Partnership (RCEP) that would include 16 Asia-Pacific countries.[62]

Cross-Strait Economic Ties

The importance of the PRC as a trading partner for Taiwan is significant and has been growing rapidly (see **Figure 1**).[63] Taiwan's total trade with China grew from $31.3 billion in 2000 to $121.6 billion in 2012 (a 288.5% increase).[64] The PRC is Taiwan's largest trading partner (followed by Japan and the United States),[65] its largest export market, and its second-largest source of imports (after Japan).[66] According to Taiwan's Mainland Affairs Council (MAC), the share of Taiwan's exports to China rose from 3.2% in 1985 to 28.4% in 2012, while the share of its imports from China rose from 0.6% to 15.1%.[67] Taiwan has enjoyed large annual trade surpluses with the mainland over the past several years, which totaled $39.8 billion in 2012.[68]

---

[60] Taiwan Ministry of Economic Affairs, *Overview of Taiwan's Progress on FTA/ECA*, October 24, 2012, at http://www.moea.gov.tw/Mns/otn_e/content/SubMenu.aspx?menu_id=6199.

[61] Taiwan signed an investment agreement with Japan in 2011.

[62] The RCEP would include the ASEAN countries, China, Japan, South Korea, India, Australia, and New Zealand.

[63] In 2001, Taiwan decided to relax restrictions on Taiwan's investments in the PRC and to sharply reduce the number of PRC products subject to import bans in order to boost Taiwan's economy (which was in recession), as well as to take advantage of new economic opportunities that were expected to occur following the PRC's accession to the World Trade Organization (WTO) in December 2001. Taiwan joined the WTO in January 2002.

[64] Taiwan's trade with China peaked at $134.7 billion in 2011.

[65] In 2012, the United States was Taiwan's second largest export market and third largest source of imports.

[66] China replaced the United States as Taiwan's largest export market in 2002 and has remained so through 2012.

[67] Taiwan's exports to, and imports from, China in 2012 were $80.7 billion and $40.9 billion, respectively.

[68] PRC data indicate that its trade deficit with Taiwan in 2012 was the largest incurred with any of its trading partners.

Figure 1. Taiwan's Trade with China as a Percent of its Total Trade: 2000 and 2012

(percent)

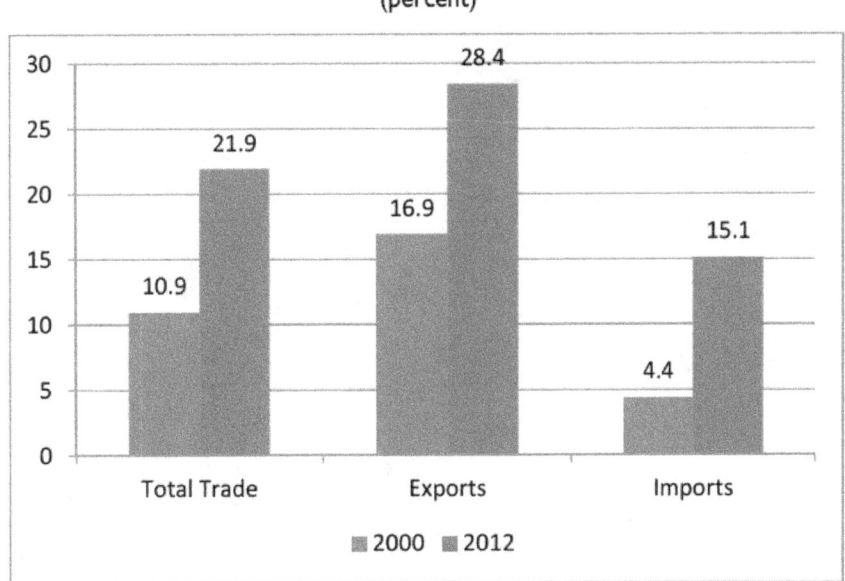

Source: Taiwan's Mainland Affairs Council.

Note: Data include direct trade as well as estimated indirect trade through Hong Kong.

Taiwan is a major source of foreign direct investment (FDI) flows to the PRC. According to the MAC, Taiwan's approved FDI flows to China totaled $10.9 billion in 2012 (see **Figure 2**), which was down by 11% over the previous year, and its cumulative approved FDI in China from 1991 to 2012 was $124.5 billion, 81% of which is in manufacturing. These top five sectors of Taiwan's cumulative FDI in China include electronic parts and components manufacturing ($24.5 billion); computers, electronic, and optical products manufacturing ($17.2 billion); electrical equipment manufacturing ($9.3 billion); wholesale and retail trade ($7.0 billion); and fabricated metal products manufacturing ($5.9 billion). Many analysts argue that a large level of Taiwan's investment in China is not reported to the government. For example, many Taiwan investors are believed to invest in China through a Hong Kong entity in order to avoid scrutiny by Taiwan's government. Some analysts estimate the total level of Taiwan FDI in China could be as high as $300 billion.[69] More than 1 million Taiwan people are estimated to be residing in China, and more than 70,000 Taiwan companies have operations there.[70]

---

[69] U.S. Department of State, 2013 Investment Climate Statement-Taiwan, February 2013, at http://www.state.gov/e/eb/rls/othr/ics/2013/204742.htm.

[70] American Institute in Taiwan, Taiwan Economic and Political Background Note, February 8, 2012.

Figure 2. Taiwan's Annual Approved Outbound Investment to China: 1991-2012

($ billions)

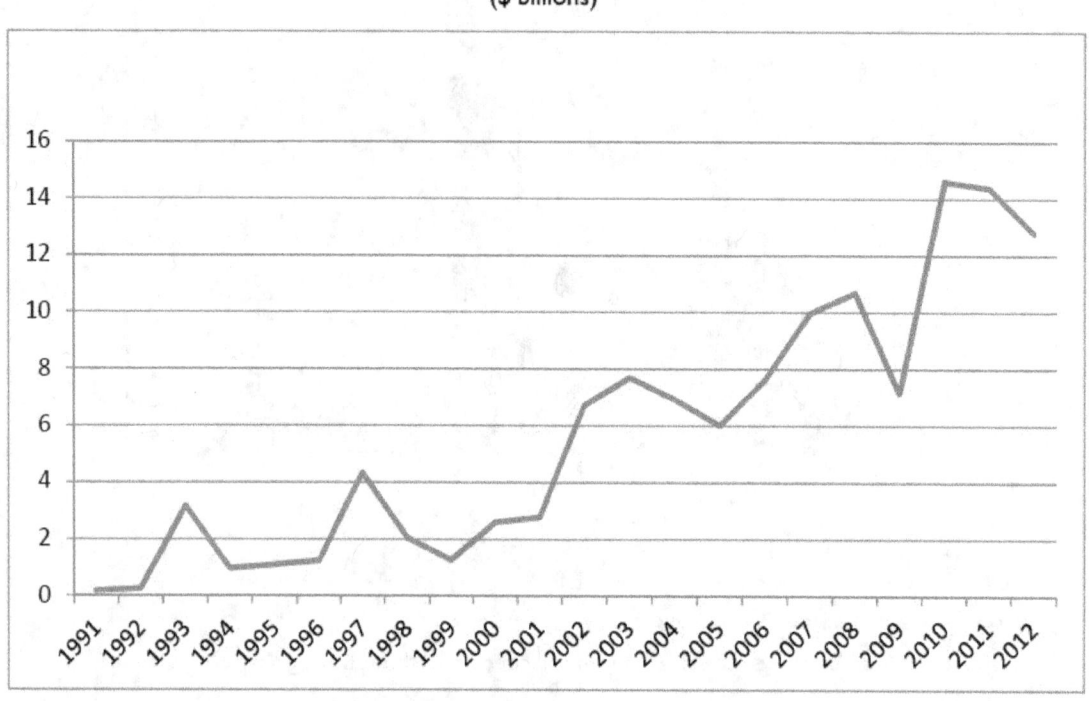

Source: Taiwan Investment Commission.

Notes: Taiwan's data reflect only FDI to China that was approved by the government. They likely do not include FDI in China by Taiwan investors that did not seek or obtain government approval.

U.S.-Taiwan Trade and Investment Flows

U.S. trade data appear to indicate that the relative importance of Taiwan as a U.S. trading partner has declined over the past 20 or so years, especially when compared with U.S. trade with China. For example:

- Total U.S. trade with Taiwan in 2012 was $63.2 billion, making Taiwan the 11th-largest U.S. trading partner—down from 6th in 1989.

- U.S imports from Taiwan were $38.9 billion, making Taiwan the 11th-largest source of U.S. imports—down from 5th in 1989.

- U.S. exports to Taiwan were $24.7 billion, making Taiwan the 16th-largest U.S. export market—down from 9th in 1989. Taiwan was the 7th-largest export market for U.S. agricultural products in 2012.[71]

- Major U.S. imports from Taiwan in 2012 included semiconductors and other electronic components; communications equipment; computer equipment; and motor vehicle parts. Major U.S. exports to Taiwan included semiconductors and

---

[71] Conversely, the importance of China as a U.S. trading partner has risen significantly between 1989 and 2012: from 10th to 2nd for total trade, from 15th to 3rd for exports, and from 9th to 1st for imports.

other electronic components; industrial machinery; basic chemicals; waste and scrap; and oilseeds and grains (**Table 2**).

- At the end of 2012, Taiwan was the sixth-largest foreign holder of U.S. Treasury securities at $199 billion.

Table 2. Top Five U.S. Trade Commodities with Taiwan: 2012

($ millions)

Major U.S. Import Commodities from Taiwan	
Semiconductors and other electronic components	6,078
Communications equipment	4,637
Computer equipment	2,236
Motor vehicle parts	2,095
Navigational, measuring, electro-medical, and control instruments	1,901
Major U.S. Export Commodities to Taiwan	
Semiconductors and other electronic components	3,202
Industrial machinery	2,558
Basic chemicals	2,053
Waste & scrap	1,720
Oilseeds and grains	1,460

Source: U.S. International Trade Commission DataWeb.

As indicated in **Figure 3**, U.S. trade with Taiwan has been relatively stagnant over the past 10 years. From 2003 to 2012, U.S. exports to, and imports from, Taiwan grew by 41.1% and 22.1%, respectively, compared to the growth of total U.S. exports and imports during this period of 113.7% and 80.7%, respectively.

Figure 3. U.S.-Taiwan Merchandise Trade: 2000-2012

($ billions)

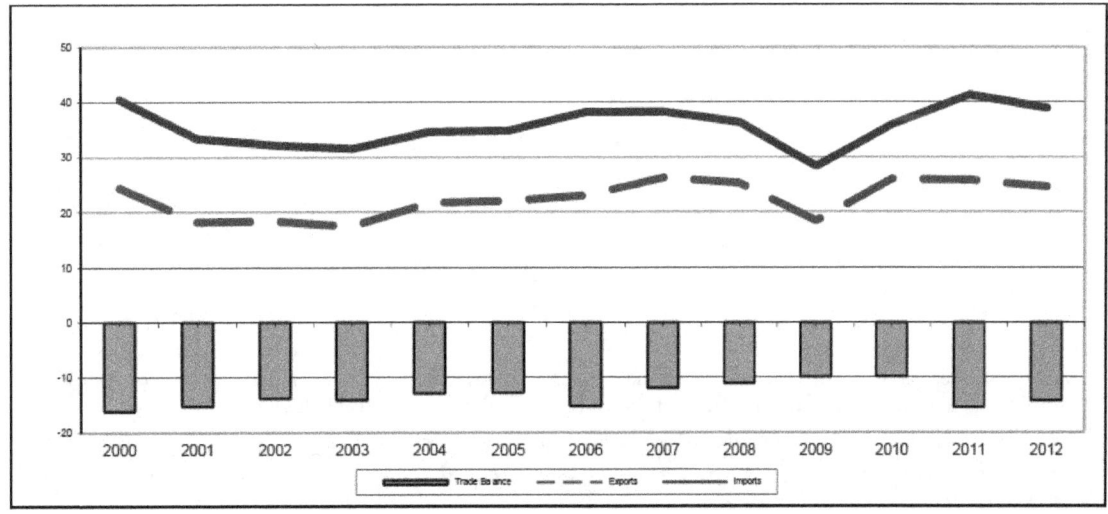

Source: U.S. International Trade Commission (USITC) DataWeb.

The Role of Supply Chains

U.S. data on trade with Taiwan likely understate the importance of Taiwan to the U.S. economy because of the role of global supply chains. To illustrate, Taiwan's manufacturers and traders report data on the amount of export orders they receive from various countries. These data indicate that annual orders for products from U.S. buyers are much larger than the reported level of annual U.S. imports from Taiwan. For example, U.S. imports from Taiwan in 2012 were $38.9 billion. However, U.S. export orders placed with Taiwanese firms in that year were $107.2 billion. As can be seen in **Figure 4**, the gap between U.S. imports from Taiwan and U.S. export orders to Taiwanese firms has widened considerably over the past 10 years.

The disparity between the data on Taiwan's export orders and U.S. import data largely is explained by the fact that a significant level of products designed and sold by Taiwan's firms are actually built elsewhere, especially in mainland China, and then shipped globally, including to the United States. For example, from 2001 to 2008, the value of Taiwan's information technology (IT) hardware (such as computers) production increased from $42.8 billion to $100.0 billion.[72] However, the share of that production in Taiwan during this time declined from 47.1% to 1.3%, while the share in China increased from 36.9% to 90.6%. A significant amount of Taiwan's IT hardware products that are assembled in China are exported. U.S. trade data indicate that computer products and parts are the single largest category of U.S. imports from China. Thus, it is likely that a large share of U.S. imports of computers and computer parts from China originate from Taiwan-invested firms in China. In many cases, U.S. IT firms place orders for products with Taiwan's firms, which manufacture the products in China, then ship them to the United States, where U.S. firms sell the products under their own brand name. According to MOEA, U.S. firms, such as Apple, Inc., Dell, Verizon, and HP are among the major global purchasers of ICT products made by Taiwanese firms. For example, many of Apple Inc.'s products (such as iPads, iPhones, and iPods), which were developed and engineered in the United States, are assembled by Taiwan's firms in China (using imported parts), then exported abroad, including to the United States.[73] According to the State Department, Taiwan factories in China produced slightly more than 50% of export orders received by Taiwan companies' headquarters by late 2010, up from 11.5% in early 2000, and for Taiwan IT firms, this ratio is around 85%.[74]

---

[72] According to TechTerms.com, information technology refers to anything related to computing technology, such as networking, hardware, software, the Internet, or the people that work with these technologies.

[73] Taiwan's Foxconn Technology Group is Apple's major supplier.

[74] U.S. Department of State, *2013 Investment Climate Statement-Taiwan*, February 2013, at http://www.state.gov/e/eb/rls/othr/ics/2013/204742 htm.

Figure 4. Comparison of Taiwan Export Orders From the United States with U.S. Imports from Taiwan: 2000-2012

($ billions)

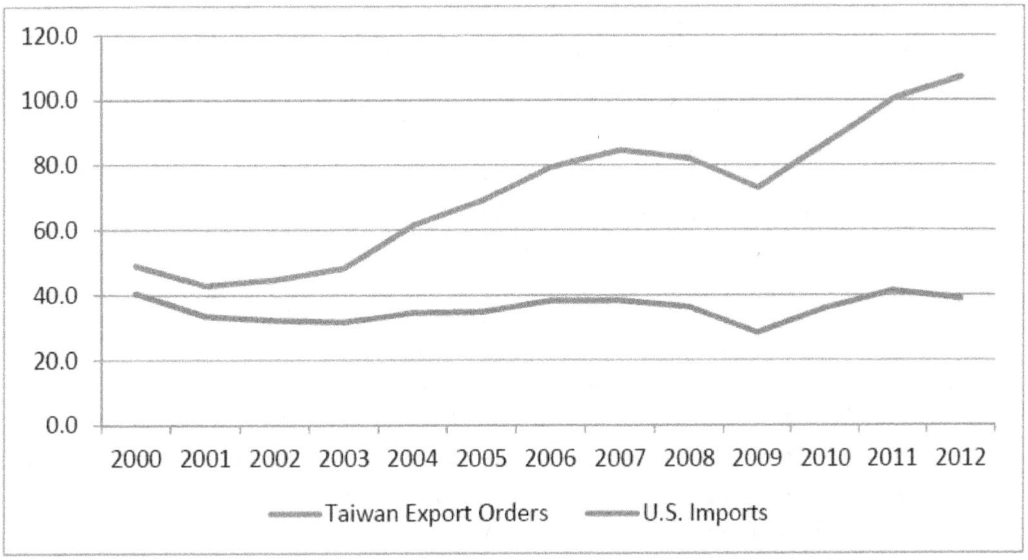

Source: Taiwan export order data are from the Taiwan Ministry of Economics. Data on U.S. imports are from the USITC DataWeb.

Notes: Export for a given year reflect orders received by Taiwanese firms throughout the year. The year a product was ordered and the year the product arrived in the country where the order originated may differ.

According to the U.S. Bureau of Economic Affairs (BEA), Taiwan's cumulative FDI in the United States through 2011 was $5.2 billion (compared to China's FDI in the United States at $3.8 billion). The BEA estimates U.S. FDI in Taiwan through 2011 at $15.8 billion. According to MOFA, the United States is both Taiwan's largest destination of its outflows and the largest source of FDI inflows into Taiwan; it estimates cumulative U.S. FDI in Taiwan through 2011 was $21.5 billion (19.2% of total FDI inflows) and Taiwan's cumulative outflows to the United States were reported at $13.0 billion (18.8% of Taiwan's total FDI outflows).[75]

U.S.-Taiwan Commercial Issues. The economic relationship between the United States and Taiwan has been generally positive, although there are a few issues that have proved contentious.

- **Sanitary and Phyto-sanitary (SPS) Issues**. These have ranked among the most contentious issues in the relationship. As noted earlier, Taiwan's restrictions on certain imported U.S. beef products led the United States to suspend the bilateral TIFA talks for several years. Although Taiwan changed its regulations regarding ractopamine in beef, it has not done so for pork. Some Members of Congress have suggested that the United States should initiate a dispute settlement case against Taiwan's pork barriers in the WTO.[76] In addition, Taiwan has rejected

---

[75] Taiwan's cumulative FDI flows to the United States, and cumulative U.S. FDI flows to Taiwan were $13.1 billion and $21.9 billion, respectively. Note U.S. data on bilateral FDI often differ from those of its investment partners.

[76] A number of other countries also maintain restrictions on meat products containing ractopamine, including China, Russia, and members of the European Union. See *The Hill's Congressional Blog*, February 27, 2013.

agricultural shipments of U.S. cherries, apples, wheat, barley, strawberries, and corn over SPS issues, which, the United States contends, are not justified.[77]

- **Intellectual property rights (IPR)**. In recent years, Taiwan has strived to improve its protection and enforcement of IPR. Such improvements led the USTR in January 2009 to remove Taiwan from its annual "Special 301" list of countries whose IPR policies were of the greatest concern to the United States.[78] In 2012, the USTR stated that Taiwan generally provides effective IPR protection and enforcement, although it noted that a number of problems remain, such as infringement of copyrighted material on the Internet and widespread commercial photocopying of university textbooks.[79] However, in February 2013, the International Intellectual Property Alliance (IIPA), a private sector coalition representing U.S. copyright-based industries, stated that Taiwan had "allowed copyright piracy, particularly in the online environment, to spiral out of control." It added that "the enforcement situation in Taiwan has deteriorated in the past several years to the point that, without some signs of positive change, IIPA members will consider recommending that Taiwan again be placed back on the Special 301 Watch List."[80]

- **Government Procurement**. In July 2009, Taiwan joined the WTO's Government Procurement Agreement (GPA), which gives U.S. firms (and other members of the GPA) access to an annual procurement market estimated at $6 billion.[81] According to the USTR's office, while Taiwan has made several reforms to open up its government procurement market, U.S. firms have encountered a number of problems, including issues relating to transparency, contract terms and conditions, and licensing and liabilities.[82]

- **Investment Restrictions**. Taiwan bans or limits foreign investment in various sectors, including agricultural production, chemical manufacturing, bus transportation, and public utilities. Restrictions exist on FDI in a number of industries, including telecommunications, cable television broadcast services, high-speed rail, and piped natural gas.[83]

TIFA Talks. The United States and Taiwan resumed the TIFA talks in Taipei on March 10, 2013, after a hiatus of nearly six years (previous talks were held in July 2007). The two sides released

---

[77] USTR, *Sanitary and Phytosanitary Measures (SPS Report)*, 2012, p.78.

[78] Taiwan was designated a Special 301 "watch list" country, an indicator that particular problems existed in that country with respect to IPR protection, enforcement, or market access. When Taiwan was removed from the Special 301 list, the USTR's Office stated: Taiwan has come a long way on this issue over the last eight years. In 2001, USTR called Taiwan a haven for pirates. Today, Taiwan has strengthened its enforcement, strengthened its laws, and demonstrated a commitment to becoming a haven for innovation and creativity. This is a credit to the hard work done by Taiwan as well as to our close bilateral cooperation. We hope that this progress can continue and be duplicated in other areas of our trade relationship." (source: USTR, *Press Release*, January 2009)

[79] USTR, *the 2012 National Trade Estimate Report on Foreign Trade Barriers (NTE)*, March 2012, p. 361.

[80] IIPA, Taiwan, *2013 Special 301 Report on Copyright Protection and Enforcement*, 2013, at http://www.iipa.com/rbc/2013/2013SPEC301TAIWAN.PDF.

[81] The GPA is plurilateral agreement within the WTO. Its currently has 15 members, including the United States, the European Union, Canada, and Japan.

[82] USTR, *2013 Trade Policy Agenda and 2012 Annual Report*, March 1, 2013, p. 151.

[83] U.S. Department of State, *2013 Investment Climate Statement—Taiwan*, February 2013, at http://www.state.gov/e/eb/rls/othr/ics/2013/204742 htm.

joint statements on investment principles and ICT services, and announced new TIFA working groups on investment and technical barriers to trade. Deputy USTR Demetrios Marantis stated:

> The resumption of TIFA talks between Taiwan and the United States represents a new stage in our economic relationship that will more fully open the lines of communication on trade and investment. The dedication of our partners from Taiwan to achieving positive outcomes in investment, information and communication technology services, and other areas is a testament to President Ma's vision for Taiwan's economic opening and deepening ties with regional and global partners.[84]

Bilateral Investment Agreement (BIA). After a resumption of TIFA talks, Taiwan has made the signing of a BIA with the United States a priority as part of its efforts to boost bilateral economic ties. Such an agreement could improve the investment climate in both economies by lowering investment barriers, improving transparency, and establishing a dispute resolution mechanism, which could subsequently increase bilateral investment and trade flows. In September 2013, officials in the United States and Taiwan held investment talks under the newly created TIFA investment working group. During the October 2013 Asia-Pacific Economic Cooperation (APEC) summit, Secretary of State John Kerry and former Taiwan vice president Vincent Siew (Taiwan's representative to the APEC summit) held a sideline meeting to discuss the economic relationship. Siew was quoted as saying: "We aim to further talks under the Taiwan-U.S. Trade and Investment Framework Agreement and push for the signing of a bilateral investment agreement en route to concluding a free trade pact." He further stated that "This is part of the building blocks approach that is paving the way for Taiwan to take part in regional trade groupings such as the Trans-Pacific Partnership."[85] The United States also is pursuing a similar agreement with China (a bilateral investment treaty, or BIT), while Taiwan reached a Cross-strait Investment Protection and Promotion Agreement with the PRC in 2012 following ECFA.

Legislation in the 113th Congress

H.R. 419 (Ros-Lehtinen), Taiwan Policy Act of 2013, to strengthen the U.S.-Taiwan relationship.

H.R. 772 (Faleomavaega), to promote peaceful and collaborative resolution of the South China Sea dispute.

H.R. 1151 (Royce)/P.L. 113-17, to direct the Secretary of State to develop a strategy to obtain observer status for Taiwan at the triennial International Civil Aviation Organization Assembly.

H.R. 1960 (McKeon), National Defense Authorization Act for FY2014.

H.R. 3470 (Royce), to provide for the transfer of naval vessels to certain foreign countries.

---

[84] USTR, *Press Release*, March 10, 2013, at http://www.ustr.gov/about-us/press-office/press-releases/2013/march/amb-marantis-Taiwan-TIFA. According to the USTR, TIFA agreements "serve as a forum for the United States and other governments to meet and discuss issues of mutual interest with the objective of improving cooperation and enhancing opportunities for trade and investment." Resolution of trade and investment barriers within the TIFA framework can often serve as a path to an eventual FTA with the United States. (Source: USTR, Trade & Investment Framework Agreements, at http://www.ustr.gov/trade-agreements/trade-investment-framework-agreements).

[85] *Taiwan Today*, October 7, 2013, at http://www.taiwantoday.tw/ct.asp?xItem=210229&CtNode=436.

H.Con.Res. 29 (McCaul), to express the sense of Congress that the United States should resume normal diplomatic relations with Taiwan.

H.Con.Res. 46 (Andrews), to urge the Government of Taiwan to grant former President Chen Shui-bian medical parole to ensure that he receives the highest level of medical attention.

H.Con.Res. 55 (Garrett), to express the sense of Congress that Taiwan and its 23,000,000 people deserve membership in the United Nations.

H.Res. 185 (Bentivolio), Taiwan Travel Act, to declare that it should be U.S. policy to encourage visits between the United States and Taiwan at all levels.

S. 12 (Coats), Naval Vessel Transfer Act of 2013, *inter alia*, to authorize the transfer by sale of four excess Perry-class frigates to Taiwan.

S. 579 (Menendez), to direct the Secretary of State to develop a strategy to obtain observer status for Taiwan at the triennial International Civil Aviation Organization Assembly.

S. 1197 (Levin), National Defense Authorization Act for FY2014.

S. 1683 (Menendez), to provide for the transfer of naval vessels to certain foreign recipients.

S.Res. 167 (Menendez), to reaffirm the strong U.S. support for the peaceful resolution of territorial, sovereignty, and jurisdictional disputes in the Asia-Pacific maritime domains.

Author Contact Information

Shirley A. Kan
Specialist in Asian Security Affairs
skan@crs.loc.gov, 7-7606

Wayne M. Morrison
Specialist in Asian Trade and Finance
wmorrison@crs.loc.gov, 7-7767

www.ingramcontent.com/pod-product-compliance
Lightning Source LLC
Chambersburg PA
CBHW080620290526
45790CB00007B/2856